Jaico Young Readers

THE ILLUSTRATED RAMAYANA

A Prince in Exile

The Journey Begins

JAICO PUBLISHING HOUSE

Ahmedabad Bangalore Bhopal Bhubaneswar Chennai
Delhi Hyderabad Kolkata Lucknow Mumbai

Published by Jaico Publishing House
A-2 Jash Chambers, 7-A Sir Phirozshah Mehta Road
Fort, Mumbai - 400 001
jaicopub@jaicobooks.com
www.jaicobooks.com

Published in arrangement with
Torchlight Publishing
ISKCON Mayapur
Chakra Building No. 135
Nadia - 741313, West Bengal

To be sold only in India, Bangladesh, Bhutan,
Pakistan, Nepal, Sri Lanka and the Maldives.

A PRINCE IN EXILE: THE JOURNEY BEGINS
ISBN 978-81-8495-861-4

First Jaico Impression: 2016

Page design and layout: R. Ajith Kumar, Delhi

Printed by
Rashmi Graphics
#3, Amrutwel CHS Ltd., C.S. #50/74
Ganesh Galli, Lalbaug, Mumbai - 400 012
E-mail: rashmigraphics84@gmail.com

A Prince in Exile

The Journey Begins

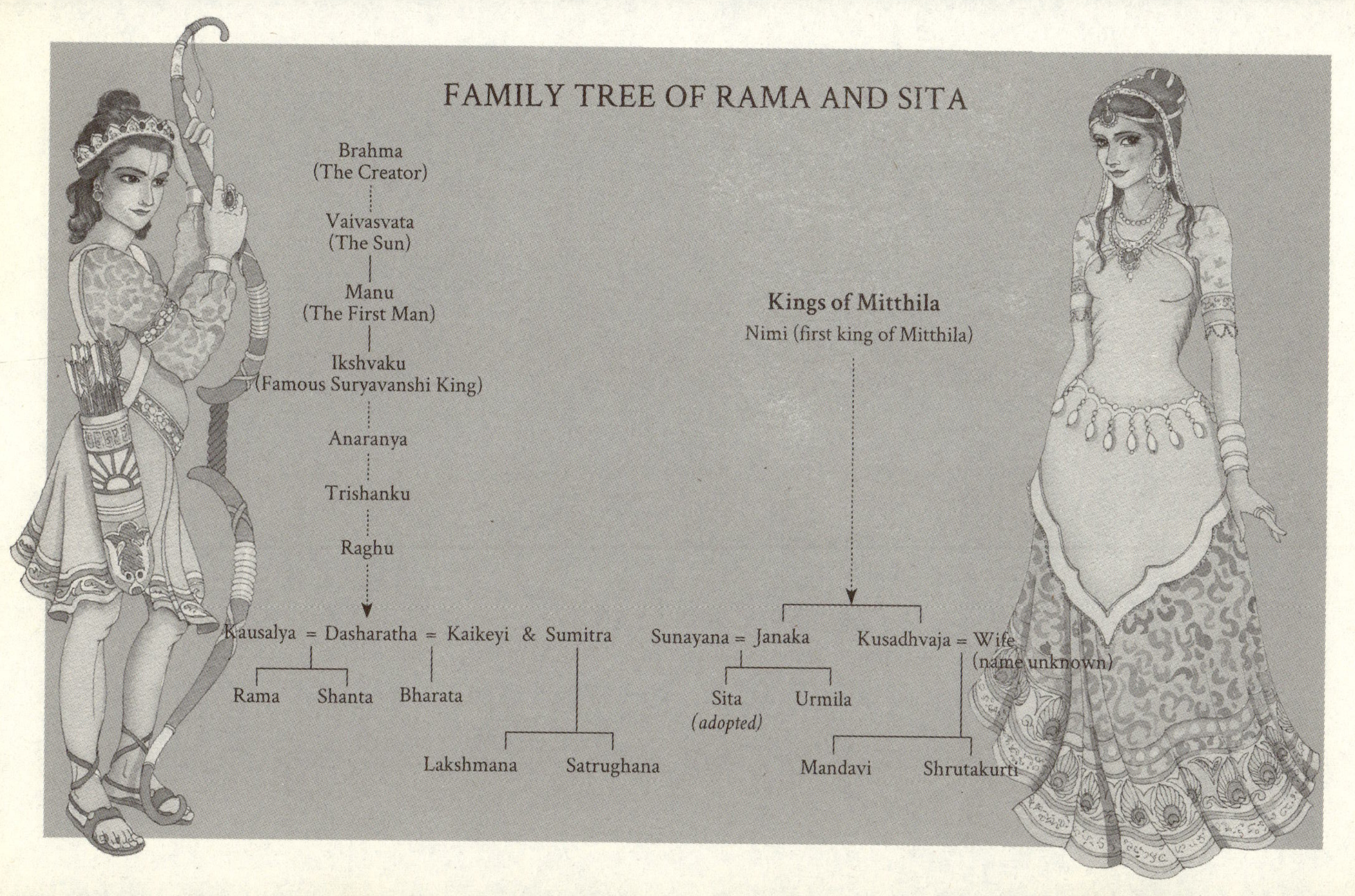
FAMILY TREE OF RAMA AND SITA
Brahma
(The Creator)
Vaivasvata
(The Sun)
Manu
(The First Man)
Ikshvaku
(Famous Suryavanshi King)
Anaranya
Trishanku
Raghu
Kausalya = Dasharatha = Kaikeyi & Sumitra
Rama
Shanta
Bharata
Lakshmana
Satrughana
Kings of Mitthila
Nimi (first king of Mitthila)
Sunayana = Janaka
Kusadhvaja = Wife
(name unknown)
Sita
(adopted)
Urmila
Mandavi
Shrutakurti

Vibhishana

RAVANA'S KIN

KAIKASI	Ravana's mother, wife of Vishrava
KUMBHAKARNA	Ravana's brother, known for his voracious appetite
KUVERA	Treasurer of the Gods, Ravana's half-brother, also known as Vaishravana
MARICHI	Son of Tataka, cursed to be a Rakshasa, and defeated by young Rama in battle
RAVANA	Oldest son of Vishrava and Kaikasi, also known as Dashamukha, Ten Heads
SUBAHU	Son of Tataka, cursed to be a Rakshasa, slain by Rama in battle
SUMALI	Father of Kaikasi, Ravana's grandfather
SURPANAKHA	Ravana's sister, Kamarupini - able to take any shape she chose
TATAKA	Mother of Marichi and Subahu, a Rakshasi, and the first being that Rama ever killed
VISHRAVA	Ravana's father, a great sage living as an ascetic in the mountains
VIBHISHANA	The pious and wise youngest brother of Ravana

Ahalya

OTHER BEINGS

Agni The Lord of fire

Ahalya Gautama's beloved wife, a manasa-putri, or mind-born daughter of the creator Brahma

Brahma Father of the universe, the creator of all, and granter of boons

Gandharvas Enchanting celestial creatures with the ability to fly through time and space

Gautama One of the Sapta-rishis, or seven sages, recognized as supremely exalted. Author of several ancient hymns found in the Rig and Sama Vedas

Indra King of the celestial region and master of the demigods

Kaushika See 'Vishvamitra'

Lakshmi The goddess of wealth and prosperity, Vishnu's eternal consort

Manthara Queen Kaikeyi's maid and confidante, physically deformed with a hunch-back

Parashuram Incarnation of Vishnu who demolished twenty-one generations of Kshatriyas to avenge the murder of his innocent father, Jamadagni

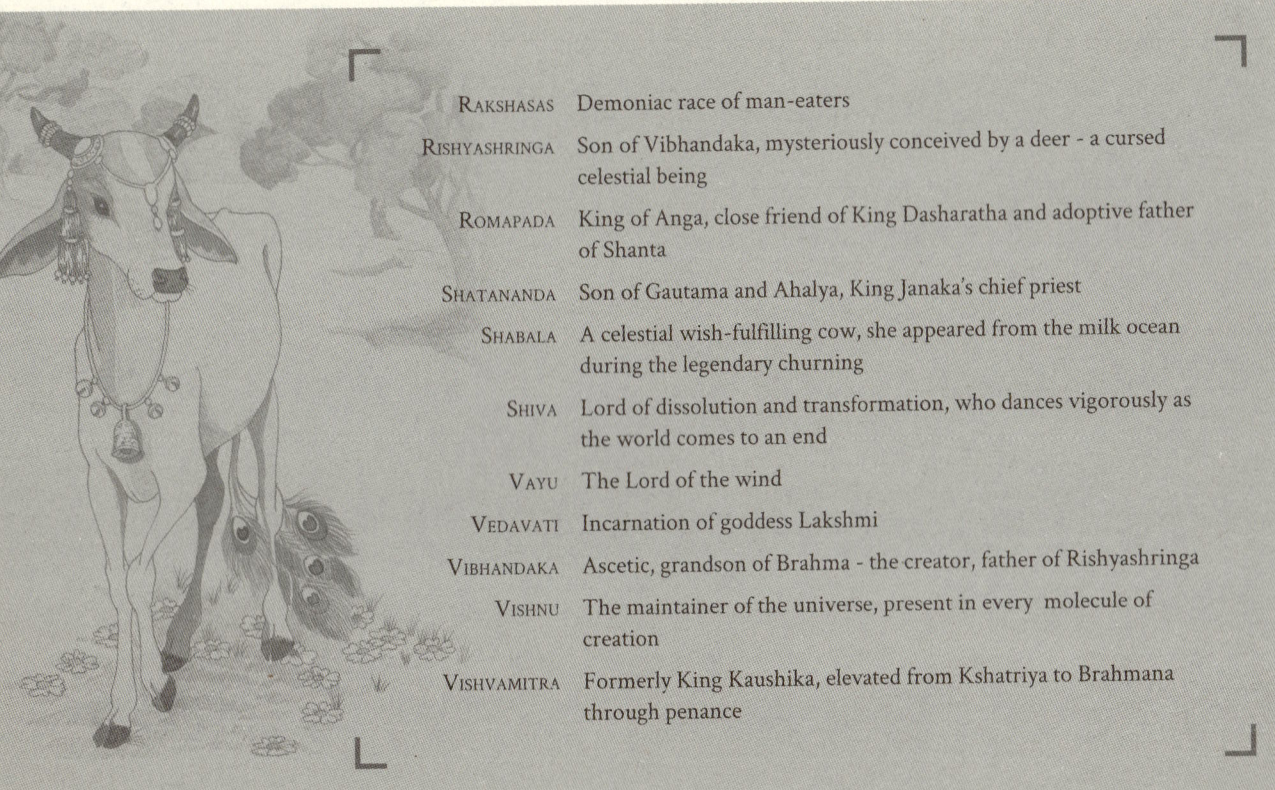

RAKSHASAS	Demoniac race of man-eaters
RISHYASHRINGA	Son of Vibhandaka, mysteriously conceived by a deer - a cursed celestial being
ROMAPADA	King of Anga, close friend of King Dasharatha and adoptive father of Shanta
SHATANANDA	Son of Gautama and Ahalya, King Janaka's chief priest
SHABALA	A celestial wish-fulfilling cow, she appeared from the milk ocean during the legendary churning
SHIVA	Lord of dissolution and transformation, who dances vigorously as the world comes to an end
VAYU	The Lord of the wind
VEDAVATI	Incarnation of goddess Lakshmi
VIBHANDAKA	Ascetic, grandson of Brahma - the creator, father of Rishyashringa
VISHNU	The maintainer of the universe, present in every molecule of creation
VISHVAMITRA	Formerly King Kaushika, elevated from Kshatriya to Brahmana through penance

Contents

The World is Tyrannized

ONE DARK NIGHT, many thousands of years ago, when saints and demons roamed the earth, a great and powerful king was born. He was called Ravana, "Loud Wailing," for the cry of terror he incited in others. On that somber moonless night, blood poured from the heavens, and carnivorous animals paced left and right. Fierce winds rocked the planet, and meteors fell violently from the heavens and scarred the ground. The sea, usually calm, smashed against rocks and sucked down many unfortunate ships and seafarers. The clouds rumbled and the winds wailed loudly.

In a small cottage in the mountains, a woman was also wailing, sweating to bring forth her monstrous infant with his ten screaming heads and twenty flailing arms. Finding her newborn a miniature monster rather than an adorable infant could not have been a pleasant surprise. With a mother's optimism she named him Dashamukha, "Ten Heads," but it didn't take long for him to become Ravana to all. The terror of that night was only a small portent of what Ravana's life would bring. That night, as the wiser humans knew, was filled with all the omens that indicate the birth of someone truly terrible. Nature's unnatural phenomena had been sent by the gods in heaven as a sort of warning, a protest against Ravana's birth. It was one of their last protests because after some time, no one was safe from Ravana.

When the ten-headed infant grew in size and evil intent, the omens surrounding his birth proved true. His actions showed no trace of conscience, and therefore he incurred the wrath of the gods in heaven. Indra, king of the gods, sent forth lightning to strike down this hideous creature who killed on mere whim. Heavy rain followed the burst of lightning, but to everyone's shock, Ravana's fierce roar stalled the storm in mid-air and forced the sun to come out from behind the ominous clouds Indra had conjured. Like an explosion, Ravana then appeared in their midst. Not even Indra could match the ferocity and power emanating from Ravana's eyes. Since that day, the sun would not shine, the winds would not blow, and the day would not turn into night without the demon's consent.

As a sort of cosmic joke, Ravana employed the gods in small tasks around his base, Lanka, an impressive island where the buildings were made of solid gold. He compelled Vayu, the wind-god, to send pleasant breezes through Lanka, swirling the women's skirts attractively but never baring their ankles. Varuna, the ocean-god, was ordered to calm the sea and make small waves play against the shore. When an intruder was suspected, however, Varuna would brew up such fierce waves that even the most daring enemy would see the folly of trying to cross.

Like most beings in this universe, Ravana waged a constant battle between his higher conscience and his lower urges. In his case, his demonic nature prevailed, for bloodcurdling fantasies and desires had invaded his mind and forced him to act in ways that were not for anyone's ultimate benefit. Sadly, for the world, this gave him the greatest pleasure, and soon he became known as the most vicious of demons. It was only natural, then, that he should rule the Rakshasas, the most debased race of beings.

The Rakshasas were a demonic race of man-eaters. But Ravana was not a pure Rakshasa by birth. Though his mother was a Rakshasi, his father was a sage, and his blood was intimately tied to the gods. He was half-brother to Kuvera, treasurer to the gods and symbol of their wealth. Ravana himself was vastly learned, but his twisted mind had turned him into a fallen angel.

Jealousy was one of the first emotions that fueled him as a child when he, the humble mountain-boy, saw his brother Kuvera visit their ascetic father in all the grandeur befitting his position. Kuvera briefly landed in the *pushpaka,* an aerial mansion, and flew back into the sky like a glittering unreachable star.

From an early age, Ravana had resolved to become the most powerful being alive. He abstained from all food, while praying to Brahma, the creator of the world. Diligently controlling his mind, he fasted for a thousand years. At the end of a millennium, he slashed off one of his ten heads and offered it to Brahma. Ravana cut off more heads as each millennium passed without achieving his goal. Only after ten thousand years, when he prepared to cut off his last head—thus giving up his life—did Brahma appear before him. Brahma restored his nine heads and granted his request—to become invincible. Moreover, the pain Ravana had inflicted on himself inured him forever to the pain of battle wounds. The saintly qualities, patience, and endurance that he demonstrated during his years of penance only made him a more formidable enemy; he had learned to completely control his mind and senses. He was now dangerously powerful because he could tolerate any discomfort if it served his vile purposes.

Despite all his bravado, Ravana was afraid of two particular curses. Many people had cursed him, but these two curses promised death, which was Ravana's greatest fear. In those days, a life once taken could be restored, but a curse once spoken could never be retracted. Ravana knew somewhere in the recesses of his undeveloped conscience that there would be a day of retribution. While he was alive, he was smart and strong enough to evade unpleasant consequences, but what would happen to him if and when he died? Who among his allies would have the power to bring him back to life if killed? He could not count on anyone to safeguard his immortality. If life left his body, he would lose all control.

The first curse came from a group of women Ravana had kidnapped. Ravana's jealousy of his elder half-brother, Kuvera, was not satiated when he seized Lanka, the golden island, from him. Ravana needed to possess everything Kuvera had. To demonstrate his power and animosity, he had even violated the warrior's code and killed his half-brother's peace messenger. Although this was the murder of an innocent and unarmed man, few even noticed it in light of Ravana's many other heinous crimes.

Ravana then defeated Kuvera, destroying both his palace and his army. Soaring through the skies in the stolen *pushpaka,* Kuvera's majestic flying mansion, he kidnapped every attractive woman he could find. He did not care whether she was young or old, married or unmarried. The splendor of that golden aircraft was soon blemished by the presence of hundreds of sighing women, their faces pale and their hearts fearful.

One unmarried young girl with large eyes trembled and repeatedly cried, "Will he eat me?" Other women grieved for their husbands and children. Each woman who spoke echoed the fears of all.

"O Death, we seek your favor. Please bear us away. What did we do to deserve this? There is no world viler than this earth with our husbands destroyed and our chastity ruined! This ferocious ogre delights in destroying the lives of others. Although he embraces evil conduct, he feels no self-recrimination."

Slowly, their fear turned to indignation. Gaining strength from each other's fortitude, the chaste women spoke in one voice. "Stealing other men's wives is an unworthy act. Since this wretched demon delights in others' wives, let his death be caused by a woman, and specifically his futile attraction to that woman who will be the wife of another."

As they spoke these words, flowers suddenly showered from the sky and kettledrums sounded auspiciously. At the utterance of the curse, Ravana lost his luster and his high spirits fled. At once, he abandoned the *pushpaka* with its sobbing women and fled deep into his golden city, shivering in fear as he remembered again and again the words of the curse and the prophecy of his death.

A mere man had been the source of the second curse. Ravana had challenged all the men of earth to either accept his authority or fight for supremacy. All earth's kings had meekly bowed their heads except one: descendant of the Sun race, King Anaranya. He was the emperor of earth and reputed to be the most powerful human. He bowed his head to no one, but he was no match for Ravana, for whom war was merely a pastime. For him, flies, insects, worms, and humans were all the same—insignificant and weak. Although King Anaranya was aware that he would die in battle at Ravana's hands, he preferred to fight than bow to evil.

Almost all of Ravana's power had come from the benediction he had received from Brahma, creator of all things. Ravana had first asked for immortality, but Brahma had argued that he could not give what he himself did not possess. Therefore, Ravana intended to circumvent this setback by requesting power over the gods, beasts, Rakshasas, and all celestial beings. None of these beings would in effect be able to kill him. Since Ravana considered humans insignificant, he had not even thought to ask for supremacy over humans. Does a lion need protection from a frog? No, the human race wasn't worth thinking about. Therefore, he had not asked for immunity against humans and had even abandoned earth and its humans after he had killed their emperor.

Nevertheless the image of that one human, King Anaranya, stayed with him. Ravana could still see the king covered in layers of dust and blood and struggling through his last few breaths. With those breaths the king had cursed him. "Ravana, you are an arrogant fool. You don't know that a man of my own blood will surely end your life, as you have ended mine." That curse lingered forebodingly in Ravana's ears. To drown it out, Ravana redoubled his destructive efforts and senselessly sought to spill blood.

To fulfill the dying king's words, and to answer the prayer of all those who were distressed, God himself appeared in human form. The life-force of the universe, Lord Vishnu, left his resting place and accepted the burden of human tribulations. Born as a warrior in the Sun dynasty, he walked the earth's thorny paths as a brilliant sun, each step bringing him closer to his meeting with the demon, Ravana.

An Earnest Wish

THIS INCARNATION OF the Lord appeared when a tentative peace was established on earth. After Ravana had left to seek worthier playgrounds, a new empire ruled by the Sun dynasty was established in Ayodhya, "The Unassailable," under King Dasharatha, descendant of King Anaranya. He was called Dasharatha, "Ten Chariots," because in battle his chariot moved so swiftly it seemed like ten chariots. As the peace spread, some even forgot Ravana existed.

A broad highway ran through Ayodhya; it was sprinkled with water and strewn with flowers daily by celestial damsels who hovered in the sky. Ayodhya was unexcelled on earth, and even the heavenly denizens who gazed at it in awe, had never before imagined that a dwelling on earth could rival their own in paradise. With its beautifully constructed buildings, seven-story houses, and gorgeous arches, Ayodhya was indeed worthy of comparison even with Indra's abode in heaven. There were mango groves everywhere, the trees heavy with fruit. Elephants, vigorous and mountainlike, walked the streets in rhythm with the drums and pleasant music that filled the air. Beautiful women decorated with precious gems moved happily here and there. The men wore gold earrings and fresh garlands, and all the residents regularly adorned themselves after their baths with cooling sandalwood paste and fragrant oils that made their hair shine.

The marketplace was filled with exotic merchandise from foreign lands, and the streets bustled with princes bringing their annual tribute. Out of the thousands of people who resided in Ayodhya, none were sinners or misers. All were virtuous and as blissful as saints. They balanced their lives perfectly between prayer and enjoyment and therefore were content with their own fortune, whether they lived as warriors in mansions or servants in cottages. However great or menial each person's task, each performed it happily, knowing that the success of their society lay in each doing his or her own duty vigilantly. Although such a widespread harmony was rarely attained, King Dasharatha's careful rule made virtue and bliss the norm.

During the monsoon season, the citizens were celebrating, not with pomp, but with a quiet solemnity, each in his or her home. In this season, the rain poured, splattering against mud walls and palace walls alike. The wind blew, making the palm trees dance to the rhythm of the shifting tempest. Although the weather was stormy, no one was afraid. Rather, they rejoiced in the rain, for it was the first rain of the year. Some children even played outside, their hair and faces dripping with water, just like happy tears. Their parents looked on from their doorways in amusement and only called them inside when the mud fights began.

The whole kingdom rejoiced in the rain because the monsoons marked the beginning of another year of prosperity and fertility. The rice would be plentiful, the mango trees would bend, heavy with fruit, and the drinking water would become fresh and as sweet as sugarcane juice. The happy citizens raised their faces toward the sky and thanked God for his benevolence.

"O Lord, let your mercy rain on us each year as profusely as it is raining now," they prayed.

Next they looked toward the palace, where a sun gilded the flag on the highest dome, and thanked the king. They knew that it was the king's piety and good rule that made their empire prosper. Mimicking their parents, the children also turned their mud-streaked faces toward the palace.

While all this was going on, King Dasharatha stood on his balcony watching the rain infuse the earth with life and his citizens with contentment. Despite this he could not stop dissatisfaction from brewing in his heart. His disappointment was a private anguish, and he joined his citizens by looking towards the Lord above. The king raised his face to the sky in prayer, closing his eyes against the rain. Even as his face

streamed with water, real tears stung his eyes and wet his cheeks. Suddenly, a hand on his shoulder broke his reverie.

"My Lord, what is the matter?" It was Kaikeyi, his most beautiful queen. At the sight of her, his tears flowed all the more freely as if competing with the rain. "What is troubling you?" she persisted.

"It's nothing," he replied, not wanting to disturb her. "It's the rain dropping on my face," he defended weakly when her quizzical gaze searched his face. "Perhaps they resemble tears."

At this the queen did not press further but simply wrapped her arms around him to comfort him. He returned her embrace but wondered at the misfortune that had made such a beautiful and loving woman the cause of his anguish.

Standing with his beloved, King Dasharatha thought of his two other queens. Kausalya, his first wife and the oldest of the queens, was always grave and regal, and Dasharatha held her in high esteem. He knew she was fair in her dealings and had never complained when he had taken other wives. His second wife, Sumitra, was as gentle and pleasant as a spring morning. Both of them were better wives than one man deserved, yet they had not been able to give him an heir to the throne. The passage of time became a burden for Dasharatha because he was the emperor; he had to have an heir to ensure peace in the empire after his death.

Once, years ago, Kausalya, then no more than a shy newlywed, had indeed nurtured life in her womb. Her

abdomen, swelling more each month, had filled the king with joy. But Kausalya had given birth to a daughter. The couple had named her Shanta, "Peace," and had then anticipated the birth of a son, but no son was born to them. Eventually, Dasharatha had decided to take another wife, Princess Sumitra, but even this union yielded no result. Finally, he took a third wife, Kaikeyi. She was young and attractive, and she had easily won his heart with her beauty while renewing his hope for a son. Surely, he thought, she would give him what the others had not. However, again years passed without Kaikeyi's slim waist altering shape.

Returning his attention to the present, Dasharatha looked down into Kaikeyi's face and felt the warmth of her graceful body where their bodies merged and the rain could not reach. At that moment he decided he had to try something different. He had already taken three wives, but all three unions had been unfruitful. Now he would consult his ministers to discuss another path.

Somehow the decision to share the burden with his trusted ministers eased his mind, and he found himself smiling. Kaikeyi, sensing the change, said something to make him laugh. Dasharatha tightened his embrace around her as his heart swelled with tenderness.

An Unusual Tale and a Solution

THE VERY NEXT day Dasharatha was surprised to discover that his ministers had already been considering the problem. The inability of a king to conceive a son indicated impiety in his rule, but the ministers stated that they could not detect any flaw in Dasharatha's duties. Still, there must be some reason why Dasharatha was unable to produce an heir. To counteract any unknown negative past actions and, specifically, to petition the gods for an heir, the ministers proposed that Dasharatha perform an elaborate *ashvamedha-yajna.* This horse sacrifice would culminate in a *putreshti* ritual, a ceremony designed to gain a son.

Sacrifices were common among warriors and kings in those times. To perform an *ashvamedha-yajna,* a white horse decorated with gold jewelry was released into the kingdom and beyond, followed closely by the king's army. The horse roamed at will from state to state, its presence informing the subject kings of the emperor's intention to perform a sacrifice. A message embossed in gold, placed around the horse's neck, explained the details of the sacrifice and asked all subordinate kings to give tribute for the sacrifice. This was the time for any upstart king to declare insubordination by seizing the horse. Anyone who seized the horse or refused the tribute challenged the emperor. A battle would then ensue between the emperor's army and the rival king, and the winner would take possession of the horse and thereby the entire empire. If no one challenged the horse, it was assumed that all approved of the emperor and his plans. The horse would return home, the fire pits would be stocked, the wood ignited, and the sacrifice would begin. In Dasharatha's case, the ministers regarded the release of the horse a mere formality since he was a popular ruler.

Dasharatha was eager to begin preparations for the *ashvamedha-yajna* and leaped from his throne. The ministers and the royal priest Vasishta were endeared by his enthusiasm, but Vasishta said, "Your Majesty, please be seated. We will make all the arrangements. With such an elaborate sacrifice, we must arrange the most minute details with care."

"Tell me what I can do," Dasharatha said, trying to quell his impatience.

"The final ritual of the *yajna* cannot be conducted by just any one. First we need to find a qualified priest to preside over the *putreshti* ritual."

Dasharatha sighed and wondered how he would find such a priest. "Do you have anyone in mind?"

"Only Rishyashringa, 'the Horned One,' is capable of presiding over such a sacrifice."

"Who is this Rishyashringa and how can I find him?"

Sumantra, Dasharatha's chief minister, began to relay the story of Rishyashringa's remarkable birth and life.

"Rishyashringa is the son of the renowned sage Vibhandaka, who is the son of Kashyapa. Vibhandaka is severe and austere and dedicated to asceticism. His conception of a son is indeed a tale worth telling.

"One day, while performing austerities, Vibhandaka saw two animals making love. The sight filled his mind with sexual thoughts, and unable to control himself, he spilled his semen on the ground. Disgusted with himself, he immediately left the place. But such a great sage's seed is powerful, and due to the grace of the gods the semen fell on a leaf. Later, that leaf was eaten by a doe, who conceived Vibhandaka's son. Although it is unheard of for a doe to conceive a human child, Vibhandaka's semen was so potent that it had that result.

"When the doe gave birth, it abandoned the child as foreign to its kind—this human child with a single antler in the center of his forehead. Not long after, Vibhandaka found the strange child on the ground. Realizing what must have happened, he gathered the child up and returned to his ashram where he raised the boy in purity and celibacy, far from the distractions of wealth and women.

"Vibhandaka was so determined to protect his son that he never told his son about the existence of women. While teaching his son the scriptures, whenever there was mention of women, Vibhandaka avoided those parts. The risk of Rishyasringa personally encountering a female was limited, as no women were known to trespass the secluded hermitages. Rishyashringa was so content with his father's affection and guidance that he never left their forest."

"How long was Vibhandaka able to conceal such a fundamental truth from his son?" Dasharatha asked.

"Around the time Rishyashringa came of age, your neighbor, King Romapada, was suffering a severe drought. Indra, lord of both the gods and rain, withheld rain from that region to punish the king for his sin against a Brahmin. Because the king's subsequent austerities and prayers yielded no result, his ministers advised him to bring Rishyashringa to his kingdom. Although Rishyashringa remained ignorant of most people outside his hermitage, rumors of his remarkable purity had spread. A person so untainted is a rarity because celibacy is a battle even for great sages and yogis. It was said that any land on which he placed his feet became fertile. Although both ministers and the king feared what Vibhandaka could do if angered, they were desperate.

"The king ordered his ministers and various Brahmins to go and find Rishyashringa, but they lowered their heads and all maintained silence, preferring to face the king's wrath to that of Vibhandaka. None of them were ready to sacrifice themselves. How could anyone snatch the boy away from under the nose of his vigilant father? King Romapada then consulted the palace courtesans and ordered them to do what the men of the palace feared. King Romapada asked them to lure the boy safely to his kingdom and to do so without alerting the powerful Vibhandaka. The courtesans requested that they be given whatever they asked for to carry out their plan and were amply rewarded in advance with piles of gold. They were certain of their success.

"After reaching the area near Rishyashringa's home, the courtesans waited until Vibhandaka left the hermitage. Then one of the most beautiful girls dressed herself as a hermit and, carrying sweets, went to see the young sage. The poor boy had never seen such an effulgent sage nor one so fragrant—and he offered her much respect. Clever and seductive, the courtesan insisted that they greet one another according to the customs of her ashram—with an embrace. As she hugged Rishyashringa, she pressed her body against his, filling Rishyashringa with sensations he had never imagined. He was instantly convinced that she must have reached extraordinary levels of enlightenment.

"The courtesan then offered Rishyashringa the sweets, which he mistook for delicious fruits, having eaten only forest fruits and roots. Then, fearing Vibhandaka's return, she left, promising to return.

"Vibhandaka arrived at his ashram to find his son gazing off into the distance, his body feverish and his mind distraught. Puzzled, he asked his son what had befallen him, but on hearing the story of an effulgent sage, he didn't know what to make of it.

"Some days later, when Vibhandaka was again away and his son began to recover from his daze, the courtesan found another opportunity to visit Rishyashringa. This time, she invited him to her ashram with the promise that he would meet other sages of her kind. As soon as he was inside the ashram, it began to move slowly. The clever courtesans had disguised a boat as an ashram! There the courtesans initiated Rishyashringa into the world of men and women and, before he realized he was even on a boat, the boat-ashram was halfway to Romapada's kingdom. When he emerged from the depths of the disguised hermitage, he found himself no longer in his familiar forest but on the parched soil of King Romapada's kingdom.

"As soon as Rishyashringa set foot on that earth, Indra allowed rain to fall. King Romapada was exultant. He immediately gave his adopted daughter, Shanta, the daughter of his friend Dasharatha, in marriage to Rishyashringa."

"O King, because of this connection, Rishyashringa will be predisposed to accept your invitation to become the priest of our sacrifice."

After a moment's surprise, King Dasharatha blessed his daughter's good fortune for having married such an exalted husband. He had already heard through his queens that Shanta was pregnant but had not known the unique stature of her husband. Then he remembered Vibhandaka.

"What happened when Vibhandaka returned to find his son gone?" he asked.

"Yes, King Romapada was worried about Vibhandaka's anger. He knew Vibhandaka would search everywhere for his missing son. So, to appease the sage, the king placed many well-fed cows along the road to the palace and instructed the cowherds to tell Vibhandaka that the cows belonged to Rishyashringa. By the time Vibhandaka arrived at the capital, his anger had begun to dissipate. When he saw that Rishyashringa was being treated like a king and had married the princess, his anger dissolved, and he blessed his son and his new wife.

"Still, he insisted that Rishyashringa return to the forest after the child's birth. But, my king, the child is not yet born. I advise you to personally visit King Romapada and ask for Rishyashringa's help."

Sumantra became silent, and the other ministers then awaited Dasharatha's decision. The king had been spellbound by the unusual tale. He knew that Kausalya would be excited to have the opportunity to care for her daughter during her pregnancy and Rishyashringa's help was imperative.

"Send a message to King Romapada that we will visit," he commanded, "Queen Kausalya will accompany me. I hope to return in a week's time with Rishyashringa."

A week later, Dasharatha and Kausalya returned, beaming, with Rishyashringa and the pregnant Shanta. Plans for the sacrifice began in earnest. At the appropriate time, they released the sacrificial horse. Only after its return could the fires be lit.

The Successful Sacrifice

A FULL YEAR passed, and spring again arrived in Ayodhya as the white horse galloped triumphantly through the palace gate. As expected, the emperor had not been challenged. The time to perform the sacrifice had arrived. The previous year had been a busy one. Thousands of bricks had been shaped, and temporary guesthouses for the invitees had been constructed. The brick-makers, carpenters, and earth-diggers had actually constructed what now resembled a small city. They had built long halls to facilitate mass food distribution, and even while the rest of the site was under construction, the king had ensured that food was provided for any traveler or citizen who wanted it.

The sacrificial arena was erected in the center of this small city. Large fire sacrifices usually required six fire pits, but for this sacrifice Vasishta had ordered eighteen, laying them out in the shape of an eagle. The Brahmins who had constructed these fire pits assured the king that the bird shape would help the offerings fly up to the heavens.

The night before the great sacrifice was to be enacted King Dasharatha and his queens fasted and bathed. The Brahmins ensured that all the ghee pots were filled and the dusty roads were sprinkled with fragrant water. Kausalya was sent to take part in the sacrifice of the white stallion. Mantras for the swift rebirth of the dead animal were chanted aloud as Kausalya approached. The sight of the dead horse didn't shake her; she was a warrior woman and knew that death was part of life. Kausalya believed in the importance of this sacrifice. Like her people, she did not believe in coincidence. That she had not borne her husband a son was no trick of fate. There was some reason for it. Thinking thus, Kausalya circumambulated the animal three times with a sword in her hand. Facing the stallion, she slashed the air with her sword, symbolically killing it. With a grave countenance, she vowed to stay with the dead horse throughout the night, atoning for sins known and unknown. If the sacrifice then proved futile, she would at least know that the fault was not hers.

The next morning, in the presence of the kings and royalty invited from far and wide, the fires were lit, and the horse's flesh was offered into the flames. The *Vedas* guaranteed that the king would be purified of his sins as he breathed in the smoke from the offering. The priests performed ritual after ritual, and the king and his three queens now sat side by side, offering oblations into the fire at the required times. One by one, the gods in heaven appeared to accept their respective oblations and to bless the sacrifice. Finally, the three queens were called forward to accept their own oblations. Although they were queens of equal rank, scripture divided them. First, the priest called for *mahisi,* the queen, and Kausalya rose with pride. He then called for *parivritti,* the neglected woman, and Sumitra, the second wife, rose shyly. Lastly, he called for *vavata,* the concubine, and Kaikeyi accepted her oblation. Their part done, the queens were escorted to the palace.

Inside the palace, they reclined on velvet comforters and soft pillows, Kausalya in the middle and the others on either side. The queens could hear the sacred hymns being chanted in the large arena. The air vibrated with the ancient mantras' power. The three of them, although silent, shared the same thoughts. *What a magnificent day!* They had prepared for this for an entire year, and they tingled with the excitement of all they had seen. Most of all they were anticipating what would come next.

Kausalya repeatedly glanced at the entranceway to see if anyone was coming. She could not understand how Kaikeyi and Sumitra could appear so calm. She let her gaze rest on Kaikeyi, trying to read her. Kaikeyi was especially hard to interpret, because her beauty distracted people. At that thought, Kausalya felt an old resentment rise in her throat. She pushed it firmly away, not willing to taint a sacred time with petty emotions.

It occurred to Kausalya that Kaikeyi was unruffled

because she was young and inexperienced. Additionally she had not been by the king's side through years of frustrating barrenness, so she would not feel the deep sense of failure Kausalya and Sumitra shared. Kaikeyi had not been a witness to the king's mounting frustration, but Kausalya had felt his longing for an heir stab her heart many times. Of course, Dasharatha never blamed her, but she still felt responsible, and his longing had long ago become hers. From the bottom of her weary heart she wished to fulfill his desire.

Kausalya knew, too, that Dasharatha rarely shared his problems with Kaikeyi, choosing instead to forget them in her embrace. It was to Kausalya that he spoke, and it was Kausalya who shared the bittersweet love of hearing his sorrows. Only because she had suffered for so long would Kausalya know the joy of fulfilled desire. Kaikeyi could easily recline there now without concern, absentmindedly twirling a strand of her black hair around her finger.

Kausalya's thoughts diverted her attention from the door, and when King Dasharatha suddenly arrived, it was as if he appeared out of nowhere. The three queens leapt to their feet. Kausalya, seeing Kaikeyi's flushed cheeks, which matched both hers and Sumitra's, realized that Kaikeyi must not be as unmoved as she seemed. For a few seconds the king merely stood there, smiling, beholding his beautiful queens as he held the celestial vessel given to him in the sacrifice. Kausalya was convinced that she had never seen him look more handsome. The golden vessel, the fruit of the *putreshti* sacrifice, made him glow like the sun.

The vessel had come into Dasharatha's hands directly from the hands of a heavenly creature. This being had arisen from the fire in a sheet of flame and had stunned the entire assembly. He was vigorous and virile, his complexion red and his mustache and mane of hair golden. In his hands he held a gold pot with a silver lid, the pot shining with an unearthly glow. The assembly had been stunned not only by this being who seemed made of fire, but also because his presence meant that the sacrifice had been a success. The pot, so small that the king could hold it in his hands, was the fruit of an offering that had taken a year to prepare.

The onlookers could see Dasharatha's anticipation, as he accepted the pot with trembling hands. When Dasharatha moved closer to his queens, they saw the tears glistening in his eyes.

Kausalya stepped forward first, her arms upraised to receive the vessel.

"Drink half," the king said.

She did so, savoring the sweetness of the nectar flowing down her throat and settling in her stomach. She closed her eyes and handed the pot to Sumitra, next in line.

Again the king said, "Drink half."

After Sumitra did so she handed the pot to Kaikeyi.

"Drink half," Dasharatha said for the third time. Kaikeyi's eyes closed in pleasure, and she looked as if she could drink all of it. Feeling the king's eyes on her, she dutifully returned the pot with its final portion. Dasharatha weighed the remaining drops and, after deliberating for a few moments, returned the pot to Sumitra, allowing her to drink a second time and finish the nectar. Perhaps he felt remorseful that the priest had categorized her as the "neglected wife."

Then, smiling even wider than before, Dasharatha took the empty pot and returned to the sacrificial arena to complete the sacrifice. The queens sat down, their hands instinctively covering their wombs, already feeling the promise of life inside. Kausalya was especially satisfied that she would fulfill her husband's desire for an heir. Only

Vasishta and a few others were aware of just how blessed she would be. Lord Vishnu himself had left his resting place in the spiritual world to incarnate as her son.

A Son is Born

THE INFANT, DASHARATHA'S first-born son, slept peacefully in Kausalya's bed. That the small child was God himself, born to destroy evil, was inconceivable. How could God appear as a baby? Even the sages could not penetrate such a mystery. Although the naming ceremony would not take place for thirteen days from the birth, Dasharatha already knew that his son would be named Rama, "One Who Pleases."

Rama was only a few hours old when, after being bathed, he was brought to Kausalya's chambers. There the other two queens, still very pregnant, waited for him. Kausalya herself would reunite with her newborn after she had undergone all the appropriate cleansing ceremonies, first by the midwife and then the priests. While they waited for Rama to be brought, Kaikeyi and Sumitra clutched each other's hands and speculated about whether the baby would look more like his father or his mother. Kaikeyi had been adamant in her opinion that, of course, the child would have the best features of both parents.

Now the two queens gazed at the child. All thoughts of whom he might resemble were far gone. Neither had expected him to be so exquisite. With his delicate face and moonlike effulgence, the boy was charming beyond words. His cheeks were round and smooth, and soft black hair framed his face. His eyes were closed, and the queens could see the curl of his thick eyelashes. His skin was a beautiful hue, the color of emeralds or of lotus leaves shining in the sun. Kaikeyi and Sumitra simultaneously reached out for the baby, and laughing, agreed to sit side by side and hold him together.

As they held him, delightedly chattering about how soft he felt and how good he smelled, both were startled by a sudden flurry of movement in their own wombs.

Eyes wide, Sumitra, whose belly was huge with the twins she was carrying, looked at Kaikeyi and said, "They are reaching for their brother as if they are longing to see him, just like we were."

"Yes, you're right. My baby's hands are pressing against the top of my womb, where Rama's feet are resting."

Sumitra smiled and peered at Kaikeyi's belly to see if she could find the unborn baby's hands. "Oh, I see them! Look at that!"

She reached over and touched the small protrusion. Then both queens returned their attention to the child in their

arms, who was unaware of the slight commotion his unborn siblings had caused.

"He is beautiful," Kaikeyi whispered, outlining Rama's lips, nose, and eyebrows with her finger.

"Look at his hands and feet," she continued. "They are perfectly shaped. His pink toenails look like budding lotus petals against the green hue of his toes."

"Oh!" Sumitra exclaimed. "Look, he's opening his eyes."

They both fell silent, waiting for Rama's first glance.

The baby's eyelids fluttered, but then remained closed for so long that the queens thought that he would not wake up.

Kaikeyi began to gently prod the baby, "Wake up, little one."

As soon as she said these words, Rama slowly opened his eyes and looked into her face. His eyes were large and bright and as jet-black as his hair. Tears of love formed in Kaikeyi's eyes as she looked at the child. "Kausalya is so lucky to have a son like you," she whispered.

Kaikeyi's contact with Rama kindled her desire to hold her own son. Suddenly, Kaikeyi felt the pressure and rush of pain that signaled the start of her labor.

"What's wrong?" Sumitra asked as Kaikeyi inhaled sharply.

"I think it's my turn now."

Giving the baby one last squeeze, she reluctantly handed him to Sumitra. Kaikeyi signaled to her personal servant, who called several maids to escort her to the birthing room. As she was leaving Kausalya's chambers, Kausalya herself appeared, escorted by Dasharatha and followed by a procession of priests and sages chanting auspicious hymns. Both Kausalya and Dasharatha looked anxious to see their son. Kaikeyi understood their anticipation, although she could think of little but her own labor pains. The king noticed her grimace and cast a worried glance at her as she passed, but she smiled bravely. A glance was all the king could spare at the time, for his mind was primarily on the new object of love, his son.

"A son," Dasharatha sighed, "my first-born son."

He felt joy like he had never felt before, and Kausalya had never seemed more invaluable to him as she was at this moment, the mother of his first son. He squeezed her hand in gratitude before his son was at last placed in his arms. Holding the baby made further thought impossible. Dasharatha became so enraptured by Rama that he failed to notice that Sumitra was being escorted to the birth room, or that night had fallen, or that Kausalya had fallen asleep by his side.

By morning, Dasharatha had four healthy sons. As word spread, the kingdom exploded in a torrent of celebration.

Thirteen days later, the firstborn was officially named Ramachandra, "One Whose Mere Presence Pleases." Everyone affectionately called him Rama. Kaikeyi's child, the second son, was named Bharata, and Sumitra's twins were named Lakshmana and Shatrugna. The king was ecstatic. He had dreamed of one son and had been given four. His role as king paled as he thought only of being a father to these boys. He loved them all dearly; yet from the start Rama occupied the biggest place in his heart. Dasharatha spent as much time as possible with Rama, and however difficult his day, if Rama was brought to him, he felt better immediately. Rama was the sunshine of his autumnal years, his reason for living. Without that sunshine, winter would prevail.

A Dirty Fight

THE BROTHERS' EARLY years passed like a whirlwind. The moment Rama and his brothers grasped how to use their arms and legs, they recklessly ran around the palace on chubby legs, tripping over maidservants and into a mother's saving arms. The royal gardens were a perfect playground—filled with huge trees of various kinds to climb in or hide behind, streams, fountains, and tame animals.

One day, when the boys were almost five, they came upon a pool of mud, a child's heaven, in the otherwise well-groomed landscape. They were sliding around in it noisily when Kaikeyi came to watch their fun. Unlike other mothers, she wasn't appalled to see her darlings transformed into squealing piglets. Laughing with them she sat down on a swing that hung in the shade of an enormous banyan tree. She was settling in and arranging her dress around her when a warm mud-cake splattered her cheek. She sprang out of the swing in surprise, making it sway back behind her. With her eyes wide and her mouth O-shaped, she faced four naughty grins.

"Rama!" she exclaimed, dodging a second mud ball.

The mud ball that had hit its mark was dropping down from her chin onto her light colored silk sari. Unmindful of her royal status, Kaikeyi darted forward to grab mud in her clean hands and fling it at the boys who were running here and there with glee. Her teeth sparkled as she laughed aloud.

"Not fair! Four against one!" she exclaimed, hitting at least three of them with her rapid firing. "And I'm just an old woman, while you are all strong young boys."

In truth, she was a far better shot than they, and Rama soon looked like a beggar boy. His three brothers hovered around him like dirty hoodlums.

"What is all this noise?" They heard Kausalya's voice from a distance.

The boys promptly hid behind the banyan tree, leaving Kaikeyi alone in the sunshine to face Kausalya. The girl in Kaikeyi was blissful and defiant, but the queen in her grinned sheepishly at the senior queen.

"Well, you must have been attacked by some dangerous monkeys," Kausalya commented, scanning the area for the boys and speaking loudly so they would hear her. "Some very naughty monkeys."

Not seeing them, her eyes returned to Kaikeyi, who was wiping her hands clean on the grass.

"Presuming, that is, that you didn't roll around in the mud on your own, Kaikeyi."

The boys were heard giggling at this, but Kaikeyi heard something in Kausalya's tone.

"What if I did?" she asked, her smile now gone.

"Well, I hope the boys didn't trouble you too much."

"No, no, there were no boys, only monkeys," Kaikeyi said, continuing Kausalya's joke. The "monkeys" were heard behind the trees again.

"And it's only mud. Not much trouble. Let them play, Kausalya," she added quietly.

"Just because I don't play with them, doesn't mean I'm out to ruin their fun."

"I didn't mean that..."

Kausalya, who seldom showed her negative emotions, looked skeptical but smoothed her frown as she saw a curly head peep out from behind the tree.

Kaikeyi decided to leave. She was offended by Kausalya, who was not her usual neutral self, but didn't want to create a scene in front of the boys.

"Manthara!" Kaikeyi called to her attendant, an old hunchback who always remained near her. "Come get the boys inside and cleaned up while I go to change."

Manthara went toward the banyan tree muttering something about being responsible only for Bharata, Kaikeyi's son. However, the boys had not been idle during the queens' short chat. Before Manthara had a chance to call them she was bombarded with a torrent of mud balls.

"Ambush! Ambush!" Rama shouted, as the boys came into view, clapping.

"You would never torment me like this if I were not so ugly!" the mud-covered Manthara yelled, humiliated and remembering every time she felt like an outcast because of the hump on her back. The boys froze at her words. They had never borne malice toward anyone and were genuinely startled by her outburst.

"No, no," Rama said, always the fastest to offer comfort, taking her hand and wiping mud off her cheek. "We would have thrown the mud even if you were the most beautiful."

Manthara snatched her hand away and sneered at the boy, hating and mistrusting his sweetness. Manthara seemed not to notice that Kaikeyi, who easily fit into the "most beautiful" category, was also covered in mud.

"Never mind these tricky boys," Kaikeyi hastened to intervene. She too had been startled by Manthara's outburst but was more familiar with the old woman's moods. Kaikeyi led the sour hunchback away, patting her lovingly on her deformed back. She looked over her shoulder at the boys and shook her head with a smile. She didn't see Manthara's over-the-shoulder grimace.

Manthara stared hatefully at Rama, as if he had thrown all the mud single-handedly. Kausalya saw her glare, and the old woman's vehemence shook her. Kausalya forgot her dislike of mud and ran forward to take Rama into her arms.

"Some people don't like pranks," she said, hoping this would be an acceptable explanation to a five-year-old.

"Do you like pranks?" Rama asked, curling his arm around her neck.

"Of course I do," Kausalya replied without thinking. She smiled down at him. He was so sweet, her Rama.

Rama laughed and then said, "Good!" and rubbed his hands on her face and smeared it with the remaining mud.

"You tricky boy!" she exclaimed, putting him down. She almost fell over when Lakshmana, Bharata, and Shatrugna followed Rama, as they always did, and ran their dirty hands all over her as well.

"Boys, I warn you," she shouted, and they heard in the warning the happy fact that the game was about to begin again.

Later, Dasharatha stumbled upon five dirty figures lying panting in the grass at sundown. Kausalya sat up at once, wiping her face with her hands, managing only to appear more mud-streaked. Meanwhile, Dasharatha saw Kaikeyi, clean and innocent, sitting in the swing. After she recounted briefly what had happened, he burst into laughter and settled down next to her. His grimy sons crowded around him eagerly as Kausalya watched from a distance.

The sour old woman, who hated mud and hated Rama, was completely forgotten, but Manthara would never forget this insult. Internalizing the incident, her heart gnarled like the root of a tree.

A Mother's Morning

ABOUT A YEAR after the mud incident, school began for the young princes. On their first day, the children slept soundly, but Kausalya awoke early for the occasion. She walked about, nervously arranging scattered toys and finally settled down next to her sleeping son. Kausalya exhaled and watched the orange and red rays of the rising sun make their way upwards.

Rama and Lakshmana were lying on Rama's bed, breathing softly. Kausalya admired Rama's chubby face, his arched eyebrows, and his long curling eyelashes. His hair, blacker than the *kajal* around the queen's eyes, was scattered loosely around the pillow. His curls looked like coiling serpents, she thought. Then she shuddered at the image and prayed that no harm would ever befall her children.

Her eyes next moved to Lakshmana's face. His skin was fair, in contrast to Rama's, but he had the same long eyelashes and black, curly hair. In truth, it was hard to say whose hair was whose, because their heads were resting so close together on the pillow. A smile blossomed on Kausalya's lips when she thought of the friendship between Rama and Lakshmana. It was rare to see them apart. Even now in their sleep, they did not let each other go. Kausalya reached over and stroked the boys' clasped hands.

Perhaps this would be the last morning she would have to admire her sleeping children because after today the boys would begin their training as young princes and warriors. There would be no more running around the gardens, tossing coconuts from palm trees, or teasing the maidservants. She hoped they would still be allowed to play sometimes—they were still children after all—but less mischief certainly would be a relief. Kausalya's thoughts were interrupted by Sumitra entering the room.

"Are they still sleeping? I want to bathe Lakshmana earlier today so I have time to decorate both him and Shatrugna."

"Yes. See? They fell asleep while playing."

"Even though Shatrugna is Lakshmana's twin brother, at heart I think these two boys are the real twins," Sumitra remarked, moving a stray curl from Lakshmana's face.

"Yes, and Shatrugna must be in Bharata's chamber."

They then spoke, as they often had in the past, about how the boys bonded, one with another. Lakshmana and Rama were inseparable and so were Bharata and Shatrugna. One thing was certain—Rama was the center for all of them. From his birth, he had outshone his brothers in all undertakings, whether in shooting arrows or charming their mothers. He had such natural grace that there was no jealousy among the brothers. Vasishta had rightly named him Ramachandra, for, like the moon, his soothing presence pleased every person. As they were talking, Kaikeyi suddenly appeared in the doorway. Neither was surprised to see her; they both knew of her fondness for Rama. Kaikeyi came to Rama's room every morning before going to see her own son. Today she had brought a flower garland for Rama. Looking briefly at the two women in greeting, Kaikeyi sat down by Rama's side and took his hand in hers.

Kausalya glanced out the window again and saw that the sun was steadily rising. It was time to wake the princes.

"Rama, Lakshmana, wake up."

"I had better take Lakshmana back to his room," Sumitra said, lifting Lakshmana still half asleep into her arms and carrying him out.

Kaikeyi put the garland on the bed, and then left to tend to Bharata after giving Rama a few quick kisses on his cheeks.

Somewhat sadly, Kausalya looked down on her drowsy son. She still remembered the day when Rama had taken his first step. How excited she had been! How bizarre now that she should feel that he was already growing apart from her. A vague apprehension seized her. Shaking it off, she smiled and pulled her son toward his morning bath.

A Goddess

WHEN LORD VISHNU incarnated as a human being, Rama, he left his eternal consort Lakshmi behind in the spiritual realm. Unable to bear separation from him, Lakshmi, that most indescribable gem of a goddess, left her Lord's heavenly abode for the mountains on earth. In this way, she would be closer to him and also would be able to atone for the sin she must have committed—would he have left her behind if she was flawless?

She decided to take birth as a sage's daughter. No disguise could ever conceal the presence of the source of all opulence, wealth, and beauty on earth, and the mountain sages came to worship her as Vedavati, the embodiment of the *Vedas*. Sitting cross-legged and still, she could think of nothing but her Lord Vishnu. She looked like a diamond bereft of light, her sparkling dependent on the sun of her Vishnu. Along with her breath, her life force rose and fell as she counted the moments until she would see her beloved Lord again. Day after day, she sat immersed.

One day, Ravana was loitering in the mountains with his Rakshasa followers to accost the ascetics. Because of the austere and solitary environment, sages were abundant in the mountainous regions, and Ravana and his followers easily found victims for their cruelty. Coming upon a well-kept ashram, Ravana suddenly felt a tingling sensation on the back of his neck, as if the most beautiful spirit had exhaled. Stopping in his tracks, he turned around. Then he saw her. He felt like a thief who had stumbled on an unguarded treasure. He could see only her. In that one instant, he became one with his heart, passion his only purpose. Ravana wanted to fall to his knees in reverence and worship the ground where Vedavati was sitting in meditation. He wanted to wash her feet with his passionate tears. Most of all, though, he wanted her to open her eyes. Her closed eyes were shutting him out of her world, and he was glimpsing but a spark of her splendor.

To awaken her, he cleared his throat loudly. She remained absorbed in her own meditation. This only increased his fixation on her. Forgetting the demons behind him, he moved closer to Vedavati. Without thinking, he reached his hand out to touch her. She was like a magnet, and his hand was drawn to make contact. With his fingertips he lightly traced the shape of her head then stroked the hair that cascaded down her back. Her black hair flowed through his fingers.

It stung him that this woman saint was not affected in the least by his proximity. No woman had ever been indifferent to him before. Not all women loved him, but he preferred a scream of horror to being ignored. How dare she make a fool of him! Ravana had thousands of women more attractive than her at his palace—women who fought for his attention. How dare she ignore him!

With his wasp-like thoughts stinging him, he straightened, grasping Vedavati's long hair firmly in his fist. Determined that she acknowledge him, he yanked her hair sharply. For a few moments nothing happened. He stared at her again seeing nothing but her, his pride forgotten. Would she open her eyes? Would her passion match his? Tension filled the air, but Vedavati did not respond. He yanked her hair once more. This time she slowly opened her eyes.

He stumbled back as their eyes met. Ravana, who fought daily with the most ferocious beasts, was scorched by the burning fire in her eyes. Shocked, he tightened his grip on her hair. It was obvious that she was angry, but that did not diminish the complete attraction he felt for her.

Vedavati knew instantly who was standing before her and arrogantly holding her hair. She had prayed to see her Lord, but instead this evil being had appeared. Her hair was in his hands, and he was so close to her that she felt the heat of his body and the threat of his lusty eyes. As she returned his stare , Vedavati transformed the side of her hand into a sharp blade and severed the hank of hair he held, leaving it limp in his grip. The ever-present pain of separation in her heart now mingled with rage, and she spoke with a voice that crackled with anger.

"My body has been defiled by your touch. How dare you covet that which can never belong to you? I cannot bear to live with this body any longer."

As if he did not hear her, Ravana stared at her with unabated fervor.

"But know this, lusty fool. I will not give up this life in vain, for I will take birth again as a woman, and I will be the cause of your destruction."

Having pronounced the curse, she gazed inward, directing the burning rage toward the center of her forehead. She uttered her Lord's name and was consumed by the flames that erupted from between her brows and burned her entire body. Within seconds, only her ashes whirled around Ravana's feet. He stood there, vacuously holding the stump of hair in his clenched fist. She was gone. His body felt raw, and he choked down a sob. How fragile and sweet she had looked with her eyes closed. So desirable. But the blazing comets of her eyes had unmanned him.

He lifted his hand toward his chest as if to clasp her hair to his heart but flung it to the earth instead, a black oblation falling into the gray of her ashes. Then he quickly turned away and left the mountains, his demon associates following silently behind. He would try to forget her; however, the red-hot rubies of her eyes were unforgettable and scorched his dreams.

Thus, Ravana, who had caused God to appear as a human being, also caused the goddess to become a part of the scheme that would end his earthly existence. To fulfill the words of the helpless women Ravana had cruelly kidnapped, Goddess Lakshmi too would incarnate to destroy him.

Lakshmi incarnated one day when a kind-looking man peacefully scattered seeds into some freshly tilled furrows. Many servants were standing around the area, looking on and chatting amiably. Although he was their master, they did not think of offering to help him with his menial task. He scattered the seeds with the same serenity with which he did everything. As this was a ritual sowing of seed, the plot had been prepared for this sacrifice, which all kings in that era performed at regular intervals. The king would have become an excellent farmer, the servants would joke later, because no sooner had the seed hit the soil than life emerged. The strange miracle they saw that day was remembered and talked about for a long time afterward.

Janaka, king of Mitthila, was seldom seen without the kind smile that beautified his face; he ruled his kingdom with such warmth. He was childless, but that did not worry him under King Dasharatha's rule. He was sure that God's plan was greater than his own, and he therefore left big problems, like his succession, in the hands of the wiser one. His acceptance of God was so natural that he neither expected a reward for his saintly nature, nor did he question it when it came. Nevertheless it was with some astonishment that he witnessed the miracle the whole kingdom later spoke of.

As he sowed the seeds, King Janaka saw the earth at his feet crumble and crack open. A baby girl appeared in the opening, her limbs covered in dust. The onlookers did not know it, but Lakshmi, who in her previous incarnation was Vedavati, had chosen King Janaka as her father. No one could imagine that this delicate, dirt-smeared girl would later cause Ravana's destruction.

Lifting the child, his heart filled with affection, King Janaka spontaneously declared, "This shall be my daughter."

Because she came miraculously from the earth, the king and his wife named her Sita, "Furrow." She quickly became the object of their deepest love, and others too loved her so well that, in effect, she had many mothers. Traveling from lap to lap, the baby girl received uncountable hugs and kisses. Even when the king was subsequently blessed with another daughter named Urmila, born of his queen, Sita remained his treasure.

The Warrior-Turned-Sage Makes a Request

THE TWO DIVINE children spent their early years delighting their parents. Sita was loved by Janaka, Rama by Dasharatha. Time passed quickly, as it always does when happiness is abundant. King Dasharatha was shocked to discover that Rama was too large to sit on his lap anymore. He was again shocked to find that he no longer had to bend down to embrace him and that his other sons were not far behind Rama in height or maturity. The king then noticed that the young girls in the palace were often found close to Rama, blushing and whispering to each other. The time had come to think of suitable wives for his sons. As he sat down to ponder this, he discovered it was quite an amusing game to try to match his sons with the various eligible princesses.

Little did the king know that someone was rapidly approaching his city gate who would force him to defer his pleasant musings. This was Vishvamitra, a sage known for his volatile temper. He had not always been a sage but had once been a Kshatriya ruling a kingdom. Vishvamitra's transformation from king to sage was well-known and took place decades earlier:

He was known then as King Kaushika and was content with his kingdom. Exploring the forest one day with his army, Kaushika had no premonition of how his life would soon change. He stood erect on his chariot, which was drawn by four snorting, restless horses. The rumbling noise of thousands of soldiers walking and talking was audible before the group became visible. The clamor was incompatible with the natural sounds of the forest, but since the forest was scarcely populated, no one could complain about the disharmony. Soon the forest was filled with rambunctious young men. Although dressed smartly and armed with spears, bows and arrows, and swords, the men carried themselves freely. They were clearly accustomed to walking around with their weapons and their superior attitudes. Many of them were proud, having been chosen to serve in the king's personal army.

King Kaushika was the master of these laughing soldiers, and he was intoxicated with his power. Indeed, he had reason to be proud; he had far excelled his peers in both intellectual and physical strength. His pride flourished unhindered, since he had no substantial rivals. Though his pride may have been justified according to his skills, he had become arrogant and prone to a violent temper. The one hundred sons he had later produced were of the same temperament. Some people thought of them as a pack of barking dogs. Still, his people were satisfied under his rule. His fierce temper and clear self-confidence gave him the upper hand in battle, as he never hesitated to strike. The young soldiers emulated him; that they had learned little about temperance or respect was obvious by the way they trampled the forest's serenity so carelessly. Many forest plants were crushed by their passing, and they left many a dead animal in their wake, slaughtering them only to prove their marksmanship.

As they advanced deeper into the forest, their mood began to change. Affected by some subtle peace, they slowed down, and when they saw a clearing ahead, they did not race one another to reach it.

The soldiers in the front slowed down, and soon hundreds of suddenly silent men were bunching up, waiting at the clearing for King Kaushika.

"There seems to be a hermitage in front of us," a senior soldier called out.

"Maybe we should go around it?"

"Yes, we may scare the sages if we march in."

King Kaushika paused at the clearing and felt peace spread through him. The hermitage before him looked like a small village with its many huts and cows. Sages sat in meditation, and two cows mooed as they were being milked. A larger cottage stood in the center, and although they were still at some distance from it, King Kaushika could see a sage sitting cross-legged before it in the sun. He appeared radiant. Whenever the other hermits walked by, they bowed with reverence. King Kaushika was startled to find himself attracted by the effulgent sage.

"We should pay our respect to this man," the king said.

"But, King, we don't even know who he is. Why should we humble ourselves in front of a poor ascetic?"

"Fool, can't you see the effulgence blazing around him? He certainly is not like you or me," King Kaushika immediately countered. The other soldiers stared at the "fool" who had broken protocol. Respect for Brahmins and sages was deeply ingrained and automatic in most.

"But will we not frighten the sages if we march into their hermitage?" the same soldier asked.

King Kaushika looked annoyed but then smiled.

"Yes, you are most likely right," he said to redeem the soldier in the eyes of the others. "All of you stay here," the king ordered. "I will approach alone."

In a moment he raced off with his chariot, a dust cloud trailing his descent. The horses neighed impatiently when he reined them in at the entrance of the hermitage. King Kaushika jumped down and walked briskly toward the shining sage. He did not realize the disturbance he had created with his dusty arrival. With his impassioned Kshatriya nature he did not fully recognize the value of silence.

He slowed his steps as he approached the sage. The sage looked at him calmly but did not move or greet him.

Kaushika felt like a chastened child standing before his father, and he didn't like the feeling.

Bowing slightly, he asked, "Who are you, O effulgent one?"

"I am Vasishta, preceptor of the Sun dynasty."

King Kaushika fell to his knees with reverence, for although the introduction was simple, the name was enough to inspire awe. Son of the creator, Brahma, and counselor to earth's kings, Vasishta was a name all knew. King Kaushika sat at Vasishta's feet, and the two men exchanged pleasantries. Both were pleased by the other's behavior.

"It is an unexpected honor to meet you, Sir," Kaushika said sincerely. "I apologize for my abrupt arrival. I never imagined an elevated soul like you would reside in such a humble abode."

Vasishta smiled. "It is often through leading a simple life that you truly achieve greatness, my child."

Again feeling chastened, Kaushika became silent.

As if to pacify the king, Vasishta said, "I would be happy if you accepted my invitation for food and rest."

"I cannot burden you with my large army, so I have to decline your invitation," King Kaushika said. "The hospitality you have offered by your kind words is enough. Nothing more is necessary."

However, Vasishta insisted repeatedly that he would happily host them all in a befitting manner. King Kaushika hesitated. How could he explain without offending Vasishta that he and his men were hardly accustomed to eating dry roots and fruits?

"My men are young and vigorous. They eat like horses."

Vasishta smiled but again insisted.

"Don't worry. There will be plenty of food for one and all. I assure you that everyone will eat to their heart's content."

Looking around as if to discern hidden pots of food, King Kaushika slowly replied, "If you insist, I will call my men."

"Yes, please do so immediately. All of you are in need of refreshment."

With a nod, Kaushika turned around, mounted his chariot, and galloped back to his men. Before they could bombard him with questions, he called out, "It is the hermitage of sage Vasishta."

A ripple of surprise ran through the crowd; they had not imagined stumbling across such an eminent personality deep in the forest.

"He has invited us for food and rest."

"What?" they sputtered, "We hardly subsist on the kind of food sages eat."

"Yes, that was my thought, but he has promised us food to our heart's content."

Laughter broke out among them, but Kaushika silenced them with his upraised palm.

"I know, dear soldiers. I agree with you that we hardly will be satisfied by roots and leaves. But sage Vasishta insisted, and I could not refuse his invitation. I want you to proceed into the clearing and form lines as we usually do for meals. Please show your respect. If the refreshments are not to our usual standard, accept it as a token of his caring. Let's go !" Kaushika called out orders, guiding his men to march peacefully toward the huts. They formed lines and sat down, some with less grace than others.

The king went back to Vasishta.

"They are all here, as you requested. I have ordered them to form lines, so it will be easier for your disciples to serve them."

"Thank you for thinking of my convenience but I assure you, let go of your doubts. Eat and relax with your men."

Kaushika stood indecisively for a moment. He was intent on cooperating with Vasishta, but the elder man's claim that there was an abundance of food made him think that Vasishta was losing his mind. The old man was effulgent and purity emanated from him. However, something was amiss, and Kaushika was unable to reconcile Vasishta's words with the apparent situation. As he headed back to his men, Kaushika glanced over his shoulder and saw Vasishta speaking to a cow and gently stroking her.

When Kaushika reached his seated men, he was baffled to see huge plates of steaming rice, vegetables, and other eatables appear as if out of thin air. Kaushika stared. The men forgot their jokes and began to eat heartily. They didn't question where the food came from but were happy to bolt it down. Puzzled and even shocked, Kaushika walked down the lines of men and saw that each man was eating different dishes. It seemed that every man had somehow been given food according to his own preference. He stopped in front of some boys who were gobbling down plates of syrupy sweets. They smiled brightly up at their king; he had never seen them eat with such speed. Astounded, Kaushika walked on and found that all his men were eating like they had never eaten before.

This is a miracle, he thought. How did he do this? Is it magic? He all but ran back to Vasishta to find out.

"How did you do this, O Sage? My men have never been fed like this before!"

"Oh, thank you. Did I not ask you to leave your doubts behind?"

"Yes, I see that I was showing you great disrespect by doubting your word. You are, after all, the greatest of sages. But I have to ask, how did you accomplish this? Do you possess such magic powers?"

"I do not deserve your flattery, King. I have little to do with the feast you see your men devouring."

"But that cannot be true! You are too modest. Come, tell me how you developed such power!"

"I am not being modest. All praise should be given where praise is due, and I don't deserve it on this account."

"But then...how?"

"Let me show you."

Vasishta, who was again sitting in the front of his hermitage and applying hot oil to his body, motioned to a cow standing beside his cottage. It was the same cow that Kaushika had seen him pet before.

"A cow!" Kaushika exclaimed in disbelief.

Nodding, Vasishta continued massaging the oil into his body.

Filled with doubt and thinking that Vasishta was mocking him, Kaushika went toward the cow. When he looked closer at her, he saw that she had a tail made of peacock feathers and had other auspicious marks on her body. When he reached out to pet her, she lifted her head and took a step back. She looked him right in the eye, and Kaushika felt that she was telling him, "Do not touch me."

"This is not an ordinary cow," he acknowledged, turning back to Vasishta. "Look at her tail! And I felt that she rebuked me for wanting to pet her."

"Yes, you're right. She is not an ordinary cow. She is a Kamadhenu, a wish-fulfilling cow. Her name is Shabala, and she appeared from the milk ocean during the legendary churning."

"I didn't know this cow existed here on earth!"

"Yes, she accompanies me wherever I go. As you have seen, she is extremely useful, not only for unexpected occasions like your arrival, but also for my daily sacrifices."

Kaushika looked at the cow again. The impact of Vasishta's words gathered force, and possibilities filled his mind. This cow could fulfill any wish. She could give him everything he wanted. His heart was flooded with the desire to possess her. This cow must become his.

"Sage, she is really a beautiful cow," he said diplomatically, preparing for a negotiation. "After seeing her, I have decided that I want her. Kindly hand Shabala over to me in exchange for a hundred thousand cows. She has great value, and a king is the proper recipient of such a jewel."

"My dear king, I will not part with her. She is my only valuable possession. More importantly, she is like a sister and a most dear companion. I shall never part with Shabala even in exchange for a hundred million cows, much less a hundred thousand."

Continuing to bargain and certain of success, Kaushika replied in an insistent tone.

"I will give you 14,000 elephants, 800 gold chariots, each with four white horses adorned with tinkling gold bells, and 11,000 highly spirited horses. To top it off, in exchange for this one cow, I will add 10,000,000 young cows distinguished by their various colors. Hand her over to me, for she is rightfully mine. What do you say?"

"As I said, even if you gave me millions of cows no one could replace her. She is invaluable for my daily sacrifices. I need her. And I will not part with her."

When Kaushika heard Vasishta's calm refusal, he grew mad with desire. His natural respect for Vasishta—and the etiquette he had displayed up until then—blurred as greed possessed him. He wanted this cow more than he had ever wanted anything in his life.

"Well, if you don't want to surrender her to me," he said haughtily, abandoning any pretense of decorum, "I will simply take her with me. She rightfully belongs to a king."

"I don't think she wants to go with you, King."

"Ha. She will go wherever she is led."

Kaushika grabbed a rope lying nearby and tied it with some difficulty around Shabala's neck. Shabala was already in a perturbed state. She moved her horns to and fro and the bells around her neck jingled loudly. Kaushika's men, who by now had finished licking their plates, were standing around amused to see their strong king struggling with a cow.

"Come on over here!" Kaushika shouted to them.

Shabala rumbled in protest as several men joined hands with the king. Her pointed horns swayed dangerously back and forth. Her moos thundered like a storm through the forest as twenty strong men pulled her away from her home and owner. She thrashed her head in Vasishta's direction and her loud cries seemed to plead for help. Vasishta's expression became stern, but he continued to apply the hot oil to his body.

The cow became furious and jerked back and forth, goring several men with her horns. Like a frightened woman, she finally pulled free of her captors and ran to Vasishta. Wailing loudly, she rested her nose at his feet.

"No, my dearest," Vasishta said, soothingly patting her head, "I have not abandoned you. But I am not your jailer. I had to give you the chance to go if you wanted to and to give Kaushika a clear sign of your desires."

Shabala lifted her head and gazed at her master.

"You are quite capable of defending yourself. Now that it is clear that you want to stay with me, do as you please with these arrogant fools."

"What?!" shouted Kaushika who had silently witnessed the communication between man and animal. "You dare go against me? I will have this cow even against her will."

The soldiers, who had all gathered to watch the proceedings, were stuffed with food and ready for a fight. Some tugged at the rope around Shabala's neck and others started circling her. Hundreds of men hovered around her threateningly. They did not realize that the same cow that had brought them food beyond their imagination could produce things far less sweet. Suddenly her udders discharged hundreds upon hundreds of hideous monsters who launched an attack on Kaushika's soldiers. Soon the hermitage was splashed with blood. All of Kaushika's men were killed. Only Kaushika and his one hundred sons survived.

The king's anger reached its pinnacle. He saw the calm sage surrounded by his brilliance and knew it was Vasishta's fault. "You have killed my best men. To save a cow you have destroyed all these human lives. You shall pay. You will not live to enjoy this victory. My sons, avenge me!"

Kaushika's hundred sons were as strong and arrogant as their father, and seeing their father so furious, they closed in on the sage. Vasishta's eyes turned red with anger as he let out a roar. Kaushika's hundred sons instantly turned into ashes.

Vasishta then got up and removed the rope from around Shabala's neck and carefully rubbed at the red burn marks the rope had made. "You are safe now," he mumbled to her.

He did not glance at the crestfallen king. King Kaushika was crushed. He had nothing left in this world. His army was demolished, his sons were dead, and his pride had been deflated. He considered giving in to his last manic impulse to attack Vasishta but understood that he would only follow his sons to death. He slowly left the hermitage, but he took his resentment with him. He was a snake with broken fangs, nourishing his poison until he could strike.

Kaushika had lost everything that he valued and was almost ready to give up his life. The only thing that kept him going was his desire for revenge. Before Vasishta he was nothing but a powerless child. Kaushika was consumed with shame and self-disgust. The sound of the roar that had burned his sons instantly to death was imprinted on his mind. The idea that he had been the cause of their destruction never entered his mind. The sage's power had both terrified him and impressed him. If he could not annihilate Vasishta, he would demean him.

With these thoughts, he followed the footsteps of others before him and began to perform austerities to achieve power, forsaking all comfort. He hoped to gain the attention of the gods. After many, many years, Lord Shiva, the lord of dissolution, finally appeared before him and granted him knowledge of all the weapons that had ever existed, making Kaushika the most powerful warrior on the planet. Kaushika's only aim in acquiring weapons was to prove himself superior to Vasishta. The passing years spent in meditation had not appeased his wrath. Now, swelling

with power like the ocean, his arrogance returned with a vengeance.

He hurried to Vasistha's solitary ashram and hurled weapons at it, causing storms and fire. It was a surprise attack, and Kaushika was able to demolish half the area before Vasishta even emerged from his cottage. Vasishta saw his peaceful ashram in chaos and his fellow sages running for their lives. In the center of the maelstrom stood a lunatic, laughing madly. Vasishta recognized him immediately.

"Kaushika!" he roared.

This puny king was destroying others' peace simply to prove his prowess. What a useless and infuriating aim! Vasishta's eyes were ablaze, and the effulgence around him glared like the smokeless fire that destroys the worlds.

"Since you have created havoc in my hermitage, and since you are a wicked fool, I will not let you remain deluded by your position. You will cease to be what you are."

Kaushika had envisioned this moment for years as he launched his most formidable weapon into the air. Vasishta did not flinch. His eyes remained fixed on Kaushika as he pointed his wooden staff at the weapon. The missile bounced off the staff and fell to the ground. Kaushika was shocked and glared at the innocuous-looking staff. Gathering his strength, he hurled his next weapon. It was deflected in the same manner. Vasishta continued to deflect Kaushika's weapons with the same ease.

"Of what use is your Kshatriya strength when compared

to the power of a Brahmin?" Vasishta demanded. "You have now seen my power, you disgrace to the Kshatriyas."

Kaushika had to accept defeat once again. Sighing deeply, he dragged himself back into the jungle and again commenced his austerities. Being the most powerful Kshatriya was not enough; he would become a Brahmin. Kaushika now prayed to Lord Brahma, the creator, for that boon. A thousand years passed before Lord Brahma appeared and assured him that he had proved himself worthy of being a rishi, a sage. The difference between a Kshatriya and a Brahmin lies mainly in their temperament, how well they are able to control their senses. But Kaushika only felt disappointment on hearing Brahma's words, for he wanted to become a *brahma-rishi,* just like Vasishta. Thus he had to continue his austerities to attain the next level, *maha-rishi,* great sage, and then persist until he attained the top status of *brahma-rishi.*

When Lord Brahma again appeared, he explained that Kaushika did not qualify for the highest status because he could not control his senses, especially his anger. Kaushika tried to disprove this statement but was tested severely by two beautiful celestial women. Indra, king of the gods, sent Menaka and Rambha to distract Kaushika from his goal. After he had wasted energy and years on both of them, he took an unparalleled vow: to neither eat nor breathe for countless days. The gods were shaken by his display of control and appeared with Lord Brahma to award him what he was striving for.

"Kaushika, you have now proved beyond any doubt that you are a *brahma-rishi.*"

"Thank you, Lord," Kaushika replied, "but I want to hear those words from Vasishta's mouth. Only then will I be satisfied."

"So be it."

Thus Kaushika officially became equal to his rival, Vasishta, and because he learned to control both his pride and his temper, he slowly became known as Vishvamitra, "Friend To All."

That same Vishvamitra was now again hurrying toward Ayodhya, capital of the Sun dynasty, the place where Vasishta resided.

Dasharatha bounded from his throne as soon as he heard the sage had arrived. He was diligent in his greeting; Dasharatha welcomed Vishvamitra warmly, offered him a seat, and promised the *brahma-rishi*, "I will give you anything you ask for." He offered this assurance before the revered sage had a chance to put forth any wish.

Vishvamitra was pleased with the king's attitude and praised him and his dynasty before making his request.

"I have been trying to complete a fire sacrifice at my hermitage," he said, "but several demons keep disrupting it and defiling the sacred area with blood and flesh. I need protection from them in order to complete my sacrifice successfully."

"Of course, of course. I am at your command," Dasharatha declared.

"No, I don't want you, O lion among kings. I want your son, Rama. Don't fear for his safety. I assure you he can easily accomplish this task. I will bring him back safely in ten days. This I promise."

Nothing could have been more heart-wrenching to Dasharatha than the words, "I want your son." He went into a shock so great that he lost consciousness for over an hour, although his attendants propped him upright and sprinkled him with water.

As soon as Dasharatha regained his senses he began to plead desperately with Vishvamitra. "Please have mercy on me. Rama is only sixteen years old—just a boy. He is not a seasoned warrior. Take me instead. I will bring my army along, and I assure you that I will destroy whatever demons are troubling you. I beg you!"

Dasharatha's heart raced, each beat marking his dread. "Who are these demons and why are they repeatedly disturbing your sacrifice?" he asked hoping to divert the sage. "Give me an opportunity to assess the situation."

"Their names are Marichi and Subahu, and they are agents of Ravana. As you know, Ravana loves to oppress the world in every way. When he cannot do so personally, he assigns others to accomplish the task."

"Ravana! No! Rama cannot face Ravana or his Rakshasas. Even I would struggle in battle against them. Respected *brahma-rishi*, I have become afraid just hearing this. I dare not send Rama on such a terrifying mission. If you insist on taking Rama, then take my army as well and let me come along."

Vishvamitra frowned, a dangerous sign, and said, "No, King, I said I wanted Rama and only Rama. Now, are you going to keep your promise or not?"

Dasharatha was perspiring in desperation. He could not say no to Vishvamitra, but he could not force the "yes" out of his mouth.

"Bu...but, he is just a boy!" He sputtered, pleading, "Most respected Vishvamitra, without Rama I cannot bear to live. Why take someone young and inexperienced when I can offer you myself and my entire army?"

Vishvamitra turned to Vasishta, the lines in his forehead deeply furrowing. Vasishta could see that Vishvamitra's anger was swelling steadily.

"Do you not have any shame?" Vishvamitra demanded, turning back to Dasharatha. "First you promise me the world, then when I ask for something, you are not prepared to give it. What is the use of your promise? Your behavior does not befit a king of your dynasty. I never expected you to be so blinded by affection. I will leave empty-handed, but the world shall know!"

Vishvamitra stood up, preparing to leave. No one moved, afraid to further incur his wrath. Vishvamitra was like a volcano on the verge of eruption. King Dasharatha preferred to experience fifty volcanic eruptions rather than let go of Rama.

He again begged, "Please, revered sage, I am not breaking my promise. I will help you. I will accompany you immediately, this moment, and destroy those evil-doers, I..."

"King!" Vishvamitra roared, turning his back on them all, ready to storm out.

Then Vasishta intervened. Vasishta's calm voice interrupted the volcanic explosion.

"Vishvamitra, please sit down. Or at least don't leave. The king will never let a man go empty-handed from his court."

Vishvamitra faced them once again, crossing his arms over his chest.

"Dasharatha," Vasishta began, "you are overwhelmed with concern for Rama's safety, so it is understandable that you are not able to see that he is not in danger. Before you, with crossed arms, stands a *brahma-rishi* powerful enough to destroy the entire world, what to speak of a few demons. As long as Rama is with Vishvamitra, he will be safe. Let Rama go with him. Vishvamitra is currently the only person on earth who has complete knowledge of all weapons, and therefore Rama will benefit immensely from his association. Please see the true situation and decide accordingly."

Dasharatha remained silent for some moments, struck by the logic of his guru's reasoning. Of course Vishvamitra was powerful enough to take care of the demons himself, so he must be taking Rama for another reason.

"You are right," he conceded. "Nevertheless, I do not want to let him go."

Vishvamitra looked askance before Dasharatha continued.

"But I must. I can now see that it is for his own good. Please take my son. I consider it an honor that you have chosen him for this task. Please be seated while he is brought here."

Rama arrived with Lakshmana following. Everyone's eyes were drawn to Rama, as he strode into the court like a lion, effulgent and alert. The elders were perpetually amazed by the inherent majesty in someone so young. The brothers stood with shoulders touching as their father alerted them to Vishvamitra's presence and his request for Rama.

"He will take you to his ashram for ten days," Dasharatha explained.

Hearing this, Lakshmana instinctivly leaned into Rama. Would Rama be going without him? Rama leaned back towards Lakshmana, steadying him with his shoulder. While Lakshmana's alarm was visible, Rama's poise made him stand still as he felt the weight of his brother's shoulder against his.

Vishvamitra immediately agreed to take Lakshmana along, since separating Rama and Lakshmana would be cruel and was unnecessary.

The farewell between the father and his sons was long and tearful, but Vishvamitra was patient this time. The three queens also came to say goodbye and shed their tears, facing separation from their children for the first time. Admonishing Rama to obey Vishvamitra, Dasharatha finally sent his two sons off. He stood at the gate for a long time after the man and two boys had disappeared. He walked back inside as night descended. For the king, the world would remain dark until Rama returned.

A Test of Skill

VISHVAMITRA WALKED AHEAD as their guide, and the two boys silently followed. They had walked along the River Sarayu nonstop, resting only as night fell. The next morning they crossed the holy River Ganga. Vishvamitra had pointed out the beautiful landmarks they had passed, but on this day on the southern bank of the Ganga, there was scarcely anything to see. A scorching heat engulfed the trio making them uncomfortable for the first time during their journey. The sun blazed angrily, and the hot sand seared their every step. There was no more greenery, and the desert stretched for miles around them. A gust of hot, putrid air hit the dark prince in the face. Rama's nose wrinkled as he asked the sage, "What is this place?"

Animal skeletons offered the only variation in the landscape, an unending expanse of dunes and plateaus.

The wind flung the sand mercilessly about, stinging the travelers' skin. A solitary vulture was the only form of life they saw; heaps of bones were scattered about the dry landscape. Vishvamitra told them of a time when the area had been lush and teeming with many animals. Now elephant tusks reached up through the sand like giant white thorns. Red gems spit out by venomous serpents sparkled in the sun.

Grimly they walked on. The boys did not want to appear weak in front of Vishvamitra, whose hardy feet showed no signs of pain, although the sand was burning like fire. Sweat trickled from every pore, and it was not until both Rama and Lakshmana were soaked in their own salty perspiration that their guide turned and stopped.

"These severe conditions must be foreign to both of you."

"Yes, they are," Lakshmana admitted frankly, "but we don't mind," he was quick to add.

"Without complaints you boys have borne the heat and discomfort, which must be more than you ever experienced."

"No one knows what trials life may bring," Rama said, wise beyond his age, "so to bear nature's affliction is but a small test of endurance."

"True words, Rama, but I don't want to be the cause of needless testing. Also, this climate generates illness. I'll give you something. Wait."

Then Rama and Lakshmana experienced for the first time the power of Vishvamitra, for what he gave them was a mantra, a magical invocation. "Say this mantra and you will remain unaffected by any climate that surrounds you."

No sooner had they parroted the words than a cooling breeze settled around them. They resumed their passage, but now less grimly and without blistering feet. The boys now admired the broad shoulders walking ahead of them. The sun began to feel comfortably warm, and they had the sensation of walking through a pleasant park. However, the spell couldn't blind them to what they saw around them; the place became nastier with each step, oppressive with the smell and sight of the skeleton-filled grounds. Rama could sense that the place was home to some unknown evil.

The evil did not remain unknown for long as one of the mountains in front of them suddenly began to move. Although startled, Rama and Lakshmana continued to walk; Vishvamitra had not slowed his pace. He seemed, in fact, to be heading straight for that big lump of a mountain, which was strangely shaped with a cloud of black misting its peak. Rama strained his neck as he stared up at it and saw something terrifying. Two huge red hollows rimmed two black circles. Were they caves? The black circles were rolling back and forth. Then another "cave" abruptly materialized under the hollows, and Rama gasped.

"It's a monster!"

The cave, which had opened, now grimaced widely displaying its sharp fangs.

"It's a monster," it mimicked in a voice that sounded

like the croak of fifty thirsty buffaloes. "Ha ha ha! Have you come here only to insult me, then? Or are you simply fond of meeting your own death?"

Rama was paralyzed by shock as he stood looking at the talking mountain. His eyes were accustomed to soothing sights. He had never seen anything so appalling as this. This humanoid mountain could speak; had eyes, nose, and mouth; and, on closer scrutiny, seemed to have other humanlike body parts as well. The nose was so large and malformed that it could easily be mistaken for a rocky cliff. The hair that covered its head had invaded the creature's nose and arms. The hair was coated with dirt and had therefore appeared to be some sort of obstinate bush or plant, surviving despite the harsh conditions.

There was little time to scrutinize it, however, for the monster was coming toward them, its arms waving furiously

"Rama, kill it," Vishvamitra barked, offering no further explanation.

Rama immediately pulled his bow from his shoulder and shot the monster between the eyebrows. It shrieked angrily, and Rama, who was about to shoot another arrow, gasped again. Something about the high-pitched wail chilled him.

"It's a woman!" he realized, horror-stricken. Lakshmana and Rama stared at one another, wide-eyed.

"Ha, you can hardly call that thing a woman," Vishvamitra said derisively.

"But how can I attack her?" Rama asked anxiously. But

reflex then suddenly made him fire five sharp missiles directly at her, for she was about to snatch Lakshmana into her gaping mouth.

"You see, she is more a monster than anything else, and I have brought you to this desert for the sole purpose of killing her."

Though usually chivalrous toward women, Rama had no choice but to keep hurling arrows at the demoness in mere self-defense. She was throwing rocks at them and bellowing, "I will eat you. I will eat you!"

Her concave eye-sockets widened and squinted violently as she sought the next boulder to hurl. Rama's arrows covered her arms and neck like pins, but since the injuries were not life-threatening, they did little to stop her onslaught. She ran madly around Rama and Lakshmana and created such a dust storm that Rama no longer knew where to direct his bow. She laughed loudly. "No one can overpower Tataka!" she screamed and instantly realized her mistake because by hearing her shriek, Rama then knew her exact location.

Rama skillfully fired a torrent of arrows into her mouth that rendered all further speech incomprehensible, although no less audible. She shouted at such volume that the earth seemed to shake and Rama's and Lakshmana's ears rang. Lakshmana plugged his ears for relief.

In this way the boy and the she-monster dueled for some time. Tataka lost an arm, then the other, yet still lived.

Vishvamitra sensed that Rama was still ambivalent about killing a woman, and he took the opportunity to advise him when the demoness seemed momentarily lost in her own sandstorm.

"Her name is indeed Tataka," he said. "She is the mother of Marichi and Subahu, the two demons who have continually spoiled my sacrifices. As you can see, she has terrorized this region, which was once a lush garden. She is beyond redemption because she became what you see today through her own evil conduct: a curse made her into a man-eating ogress."

Rama remained unconvinced. "All I have ever been taught prevents me from killing a woman," he said.

"O mighty prince, to kill a woman pure at heart is indeed a great sin but to think of this monster as a woman is sheer folly and cowardice. A monster has no gender; it is an abomination. This creature is guilty of every sinful act ever conceived. To be patient with her is not a virtue. Keeping these facts in mind and to unburden the earth, I order you to kill her."

Rama had listened intently to the sage's words while remaining alert to Tataka's advances. With the same speed that he shot his arrows, he weighed the arguments and instantly accepted their judiciousness.

"Noble sage, my doubts have been removed. Your command is like my father's. Obeying you is a virtue in itself."

A steely resolve became visible on his face as Rama

prepared himself to kill the demoness. The prince began to release arrows at such a speed that it was impossible to know when he shot one arrow and when he reached for another. When Tataka remained out of sight, young Rama impressed the gods when he took out a long arrow and aimed at the sound he heard.

The sharp arrow flew straight into Tataka's black heart. She fell to the ground with a crash and a final scream as her life escaped her hideous body. Blood flowed copiously from all her wounds, including her mouth, turning the desert red. The trio left the place amid heavenly showers of flowers.

Rama had never before taken a life. The lethal weapon, his aloe-wood bow smeared with saffron, now again rested quietly on his shoulders as his feet, smeared with Tataka's blood, left red footprints behind him. With the first arrow that pricked Tataka's leathered skin, what had once been a toy used to show off his marksmanship, became a weapon. He passed this gruesome test with undeniable skill.

As their feet were gradually cleansed by the sand, Vishvamitra looked back, searching Rama's face for remorse at his first killing. No doubt it was the duty of a warrior to slaughter, but even the bravest warrior had to become inured to killing. Taking a life created no easy burden. Even though Rama's face was untroubled, Vishvamitra decided that they should break for the day and relax from the tension of the battle. They stopped under a large tree, and while the boys put down their weapons, Vishvamitra sat down, leaning against the tree-trunk.

If Tataka's death was still on the boys' minds, Vishvamitra hoped to distract them with a story. "I will tell you about the vainest man this world has ever seen," he said.

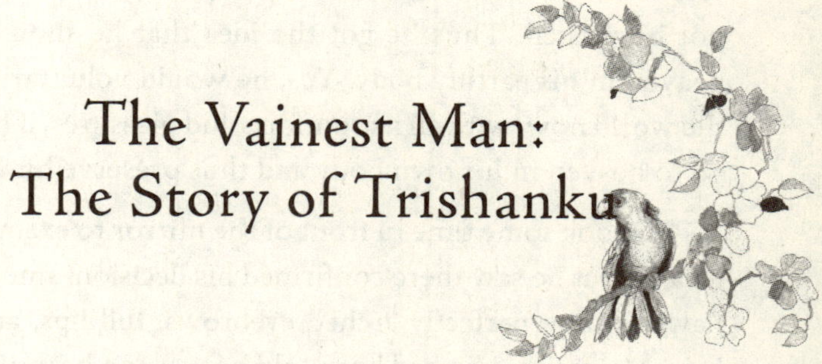

The Vainest Man: The Story of Trishanku

HE WAS REPUTED to be of uncommon beauty, and he developed some conceited ideas about his posterity. He came to me only after consulting Vasishta, your preceptor. I took pity on him, maybe because in my younger days I foolishly strove to prove myself Vasistha's equal, if not his superior. But let me start from the beginning."

"The proud man's name was Trishanku of the Ikshvaku dynasty, king of the same region your father now rules. He was, in fact, your ancestor. He was a likeable king, no doubt, and was pious enough, but he was interested primarily in his reflection. It was said that mirrors adorned all four walls of his private chambers. People tend to equate beauty with all things good, so it is not surprising, perhaps, that his people liked him although he spent more time combing his hair than tending to the kingdom.

"When the time came for Trishanku to leave this world, or rather, when he first began to consider his own death, he concluded that after a lifetime of pampering, his body should not be wasted. Thus he got the idea that he should go to heaven in his earthly body. Yes, he would voluntarily leave the world now, with all its comforts and pleasures, if he could go to heaven in his own body and thus preserve his beauty.

"He took some time in front of the mirror to examine this idea. What he saw there confirmed his decision: smooth and flawless skin, perfectly arched eyebrows, full lips, and silky hair. Many times he had been told he was too beautiful to be a man. Why not then become a god? Yes, going to heaven and becoming one of the gods in his physical body could be done—should be done. After coming to this decision, he spent a few subsequent hours posing in front of the mirror to strengthen his resolve. He decided to ask Vasishta, who was already the family guru of your dynasty, if he could arrange a heavenly ascent with his earthly body. His body was not of common stock; surely Vasistha would find transferring such a beautiful specimen of humanity to the heavenly realms an easy task.

"The next morning Vasishta saw the well-groomed Trishanku strutting into his ashram like a peacock. Self-absorbed and conceited, he carried his nose so high up in the air Vasishta must have been surprised that Trishanku didn't trip over the tree roots as he approached."

As dusk set in around the trio, Vishvamitra's speech enraptured the two youngsters with the tale, which then gained a life of its own:

Trishanku spoke as if he were already a god, "O best among the sages, I have chosen you to assist me in a heavenly task."

He widened his smile, showing off his teeth. Trishanku arched his back and played with a green leaf dangling from a nearby tree. Vasishta's penetrating gaze seemed to flatter him.

Vain as he was, Trishanku eyed the sage and decided that Vasishta looked ancient but well-preserved.

"Yes, if I ever become your age, I do hope I'll have such a bountiful beard as yours."

"No one can escape old age and death, my son."

"Oh, but that's exactly why I am here!"

He stopped speaking for a moment to adjust his silk shawl and then stretched out both arms in a pose that would enable the sage to fully appreciate his physical attributes.

"I have come here to request that you send me to the heavenly realms in the body I have now."

Vasishta gazed at him intently then asked slowly, "You want what?"

"Please forgive me for being so frank," Trishanku said, looking exceedingly pleased, "but the situation calls for honesty. As you can see, I am unusually attractive."

"Hmmm."

"But I am concerned because I have reached my peak. I'm

like a fruit ready for plucking. ”

“And you have no desire to hang on to the tree of this world and rot on its branches.” Vasishta finished for him icily.

“Yes!” Trishanku cried, “You understand me completely. I did right in choosing you for this delicate task.”

“It certainly would be an unprecedented undertaking,” Vasisha assented. As the royal preceptor, Vasishta was the most likely Brahmin to handle any sacrifice the king wished to conduct. “However, great sages strive decades, if not lifetimes, to break free from the cycle of birth, old-age, and death. What makes you think you are eligible for heaven alone, what to speak of attaining it in your current body?”

“Well, each person must utilize their God-given gifts. The sages have fortitude, while I have physical beauty. But I need your help.”

Vasishta closed his eyes for a moment then looked at the king. How could he best explain commonly accepted facts to this naïve child standing in front of him. “Let me be clear. This earth is governed by certain laws of nature. All who are born on this earth are bound by these laws and cannot but abide by them. How can you think yourself above these laws? Your vanity has blinded you.”

“No!” Trishanku rebutted, “It’s not vanity but reality. I want to preserve the beauty I have been given. It is my duty.”

Vasishta shook his head but remained silent.

Trishanku tapped his feet impatiently. "Most respected Vasishta, I don't have time to stand here forever."

"No, you might grow old," Vasishta replied.

"Yes, I must prevent that tragedy. So you will help me? There are always exceptions to any rule."

"Your vanity and bodily attachment will be your undoing. I would like to advise you to give up your folly and to pursue a more worthwhile goal," Vasishta answered evenly. "Now leave my ashram at once before I lose my patience with all this childishness."

"But, Master, I feel strongly that this is worthwhile. Please help me."

"You have heard my final word on the subject. If you pursue this, you will meet with ruin."

"I must disagree. I shall approach another priest then," Trishanku retorted haughtily.

Pouting, Trishanku left the ashram. This was a setback in his plans, but he decided to approach Vasishta's one hundred sons next. Trishanku felt wronged by the sage's brusque dismissal. What was wrong with appreciating oneself?

"That body is not your self!" Vasishta's sons sneered when they heard Trishanku's request.

"Why, I'm not only doing this for myself," Trishanku pleaded with them, "I'm setting a new standard that will enable others in my position to do the same. I know my demand is unconventional, but after accomplishing this, others will have an easier time following in my footsteps."

"We hope there are no others as foolish as you."

Unperturbed, Trishanku continued.

"Even one of you might want to follow my lead. Although, if you don't mind me saying so, my case appears a bit stronger than yours because of my looks."

His speech was greeted by the stony silence of Vasishta's one hundred sons. Trishanku had already breeched sacred etiquette by ignoring his guru's advice. "Shame, shame," they muttered among themselves.

Trishanku, on the other hand, was unaware of how pompous he sounded. "So what do you think, young sages? Can you do what your father could not?"

At this condescending comment about their father, the group of sons exploded.

"Our father is more than capable of fulfilling your foolish wish. You do not even deserve his attention, what to speak of his favor. What kind of low-class fool are you? You come begging to us when our father has already advised you against this."

Trishanku was stricken by their vehemence. He failed to understand the source of their fury. They looked at him up and down, surveying his matching clothing and his styled hair. "Your body certainly covers the fool you actually are."

Baffled, he patted his head nervously. He hadn't counted on so much opposition in one day. Their words increased his anxiety, for he did not want to part with his body. He would not.

"For the world to see the truth of your character and to punish your deceptive nature, we curse you to become a *chandala*, an untouchable dog-eater."

Trishanku was powerless as his fair glowing skin gradually turned black, his fine arched eyebrows thickened considerably, and his curls became matted. His teeth cracked and became yellow and stained. His eyes became bloodshot and lost their sparkle, although this may have been due to sorrow as the curse took effect and he realized what he was losing. Trishanku spoke in a choked voice—a voice that was not his own, so hoarse and foreign did it sound.

"You have taken my beauty. You have taken all my beauty away."

"Yes," they replied, cool with disapproval. "Now we hope you abandon your insane plan and your futile attachment to the body that never really was you."

Tears rolled down Trishanku's blackened cheeks as he noticed his dirty fingernails and swarthy complexion. He twisted his shawl desperately around his neck to calm the choking sensation in his throat. Even his garland had turned to dust, smudging his body grey. "You have taken away my beauty," he repeated through his tears, "but don't think I was simply a beautiful fool. You can't change my will. Although you have changed my appearance, I will not abandon my plan."

Rolling their eyes in disgust, Vasishta's sons said, "Just leave this place. Go now, before you further incite our wrath."

Trishanku walked away slowly, dragging his feet, the youthful spring in his step gone. Where could he possibly go now?

He started to make his way to Vishvamitra's ashram. Looking more deformed than ever, with a swarm of flies harassing him, he dragged himself slowly forward, halting before the reputed sage. It was not exactly a coincidence that brought him to Vishvamitra. Most knew that no love was lost between the two sages and that Vishvamitra's one-sided rivalry was the foundation of this feud. If anyone was apt to take up a challenge rejected by Vasishta, it was Vishvamitra. Trishanku indeed was no fool. He was quick to point out his preceptor's name to Vishvamitra.

"Before you send me away, mistakenly thinking me a wretched untouchable, please hear my story. Hear what happened to me at the hands of Vasishta."

Struck by both the plea and the mention of his rival, Vishvamitra said, "Speak."

Trishanku related the cause of his condition and exclaimed, "If you could have only seen me, then you would have understood! If only you knew how handsome I was."

He ended his story with the cry, "Do you realize that even my family and friends abandoned me when they saw what I had become? These people used to kiss my fingernails. And oh, what beautiful fingernails they were. But now look!" And Trishanku held up his blackened stubs.

Vishvamitra was indignant. How could Vasishta and his sons reject the poor king so hastily and punish him so severely for a sin of which every human being was guilty, the sin of self-love? He felt a self-righteous anger course through him, and he became determined to right this wrong. He felt especially determined because the wrong had been perpetrated by Vasishta. Had Vishvamitra not been burning with the desire to prove himself Vasishta's equal, he may not have taken pity on the once-beautiful king, but now he embraced him. He didn't ask Trishanku why he so much wanted to be immortalized in his current repulsive form. It didn't matter to him; he would prove himself mightier than Vasishta.

"Don't worry, Trishanku," he consoled, "I will do what others have denied. Come tomorrow morning at sunrise after bathing in a holy river."

"Yes, yes! Thank you!"

He slouched away, very much like a flea-bitten dog, and Vishvamitra disappeared in a rush to invite other sages to witness the event.

The next morning as the sun rose, Trishanku approached to find an impressive gathering of sages with matted hair knots. The truth was that most sages were too afraid of the temperamental Vishvamitra to decline his invitation, especially because it had been delivered like a command.

Vishvamitra did indeed pronounce a curse on those who had been invited but who had chosen not to come. These had taken Vasishta's side, agreeing that it was against *Vedic* injunction to help Trishanku, especially since his own guru had rejected him. Vasishta, of course, was absent, but Vishvamitra was determined that Vasishta would hear of Trishanku's success.

Vishvamitra now sat in the center of the gathering close to an already blazing fire pit. Three horizontal white lines of ash adorned his forehead, and he looked most impressive as he poured ghee into the flames and chanted the sacred mantras in a strong, clear voice. When Trishanku arrived, Vishvamitra raised his eyebrows then stood up, ordering the sages to take their places at the sacrifice. Immediately the gathering took up the hymn where he had left off. The sound of so many assembled sages chanting in unison was heard from afar.

"Come," Vishvamitra said, grabbing Trishanku's elbow and guiding him to a platform in front of the fire. "Everything is ready."

Trishanku stood there nervously and expectantly. He felt the powerful hymns surge through his body. Vishvamitra sat down again, crossed his legs, and half-shut his eyes. His eyebrows drew together in concentration. The earth beneath Trishanku's feet appeared in his meditation. "Rise," he thought.

Trishanku yelped as he shot into the sky. The sages jerked their heads up with a communal exclamation of amazement. Higher and higher he went. Soon Trishanku was no more than a black dot in the sky. Then he was gone. Vishvamitra, whose mental power was propelling the man forward, felt the earth's atmosphere pulling at Trishanku. His brow furrowed deeply. Trishanku, in turn, felt an almost unbearable weight pressing on his brain and internal organs until, with a whoosh, he left the earth's gravitational field and found himself in outer space.

Within seconds he saw ahead of him a sparkling planet and realized it was his destination. Vishvamitra, sitting on Earth, felt Trishanku approach heaven and slowed the speed of his human missile. Trishanku felt like a puppet as he was flipped over in one fast move, enabling him to land on his feet.

Trishanku's approach did not go unnoticed in the heavenly sphere. Hundreds of beautiful maidens were now pointing at him as he flew through their sky. It was not unusual to see people falling from the sky; sages like Narada had free access to their realm. However, this was not Narada. Who was this? They had never seen such an appalling figure.

Trishanku was unaware of their incredulous stares, for he was about to land. He hovered above the ground for a second before his feet made contact with firm terrain immediately outside Indra's palace gates. Trishanku felt another great whoosh as Vishvamitra's mental energy left him. He understood he was alone. He was in heaven, as he had requested.

Back on Earth, Vishvamitra opened his eyes, and the crowd fell silent.

He sat motionless, staring straight ahead, and then declared, "Trishanku is in heaven."

Murmurs of appreciation arose from the crowd. Most thought it was a ridiculous undertaking; yet it had still been impressive to see Trishanku shoot into the sky by way of Vishvamitra's endeavor. The crowd then dispersed, complimenting Vishvamitra on his accomplishment.

Suddenly, a loud, unearthly screech was heard from the sky, and a black crow appeared shouting Vishvamitra's name. The dispersing sages froze. What was this? But it was no crow. It was Trishanku falling head first, arms flailing. What a pathetic sight. Suppressed laughter blended with Trishanku's shrieks.

"Aaahhh! Help! Help!"

Vishvamitra understood immediately what had transpired. Indra, king of the gods, had rejected the untouchable king and flung him back to Earth. Vishvamitra's eyes turned red with anger. He ordered ominously, "Go back."

Trishanku flipped around a few times and vanished from sight. His brain was now dizzy from fighting Earth's gravity. Blood pounded through his head as he once again traveled the space path devised by Vishvamitra. The sage stood defiantly, looking at the sky. No one in the gathering moved. Minutes passed, and when Trishanku remained out of sight, Vishvamitra seemed to relax. However the interplanetary ballgame continued—Trishanku once again appeared as a black dot among the white clouds. Vishvamitra's face distended with anger. “Stop!” he roared.

Trishanku froze in the sky, hanging upside down, arms dangling.

Vishvamitra stood looking at Trishanku. That Indra rejected Trishanku, he could accept, for the man was indeed filthy. But how dare he cross Vishvamitra? Vishvamitra had not forgotten Indra's many attempts to ruin his meditation. It was Indra's habit to disturb any sage who was gaining power through austerities. He always felt threatened that a sage from Earth would become more powerful than he and take his throne. Vishvamitra had worried him, and Indra had therefore sent his favorite damsel, Menaka, to tempt him away from his meditation. Vishvamitra had wasted ten precious years with that deceitful yet dutiful damsel before realizing he had fallen for one of Indra's ploys. He had sent a trembling Menaka away unharmed, although he felt immensely angry with Indra. He had then taken up his meditation with renewed vigor. Indra had next sent Rambha. Vishvamitra wasted only ten seconds on her. Unfortunately, those ten seconds had been enough to literally petrify the woman, making her a lovely statue. Vishvamitra cursed himself for losing his temper and thus his acquired merit, but once again he had taken up his meditation, not caring for Indra's attempts any longer. Vishvamitra now decided that Indra had crossed him one too many times.

“You thought me a rival, Indra,” he shouted, “and thus you thwarted my penance. I never retaliated. But enough is enough.”

By now Trishanku, who had regained consciousness from his intergalactic travels, felt his blood throbbing between his temples. He was so miserable that he began to consider the folly of his plan for the first time.

He cried out to Vishvamitra, "Please let me down!"

"No!"

"I don't want heaven anymore. Just let me down. Please!"

"No! Indra and his heaven have rejected you, but I will make good my promise to you."

Looking around at the gaping sages, Vishvamitra thundered, "I will create a new heaven. I will create another Indra, a better one. Trishanku, you will get your heaven."

The attending ascetics beheld Vishvamitra's unprecedented attempt in awe. Vishvamitra was, in fact, doing something only Brahma, the creator, had the power to do—he was creating a new galaxy. The sky became dark and the earth rumbled as the universe creaked to make space for a new sun, moon, and heaven. Indra appeared next to Trishanku, who still hung upside down in the sky. He looked mortally afraid.

"Vishvamitra, please stop. I beg you. I will take Trishanku back with me. But please stop this endeavor."

"It's too late, Indra," Vishvamitra replied, perspiring from his efforts. "Creation on all levels has already begun. A new Indra is being created at this moment."

Only a man in power, afraid of losing the same, can understand the extreme anxiety Indra experienced at hearing these words. His anxiety was soon muffled, however, as all saw that Vishvamitra's countenance was changing. His face turned pale, then reddened again, as if he were exerting the last of his life-force. He fell on his knees. It looked as if he was shouldering the world on his back—which indeed he was. Being a creator was an unnatural role for anyone but Brahma, and Vishvamitra was now facing the fact that maintaining such a creation was draining him of all his power, of his very life. The new galaxy was siphoning his life force to stabilize itself. Vishvamitra had no more power. In that moment, Vishvamitra did what every mortal must do in extreme distress—he turned to God. Gasping for breath, he called God's name. At that moment Vishvamitra realized how tiny he was in the face of the universe. Despite his power and extraordinary mental faculties, he was nothing compared to the Almighty. Vishvamitra's eyes rolled furiously and foam flowed from his mouth as he struggled to keep his creation alive and to save the chaos its collapse would cause.

"O Vishnu! My Lord! Save me! Help me! I ask not for this arrogant fool, but to save this universe I have created. Vishnu, O Vishnu!"

Appearing as a calming feeling in everyone's heart, the Lord of lords, maintainer of the worlds, spoke directly to the laboring Vishvamitra. "You shall never in the future play a role not assigned to you. You have proved your greatness in creating this new world, but maintenance is always the most demanding of tasks. I will deal with the planets you have created. Don't forget that your pride would have led you to a sure death. Be at peace."

Instantly, the burden left Vishvamitra's body, and he lay panting on the ground for some moments. The grass felt soft, and the blue of the sky seemed a new marvelous color. The birds gliding by were so serene, but who on earth was that fool hanging upside down in the sky? Then it all came back.

"Trishanku!" he called out, leaping to his feet.

Still hovering next to Trishanku, Indra and the assembled sages were silent. Vishvamitra saw the situation differently then, his perspective shifted by his close encounter with death. Getting Trishanku to heaven no longer seemed important. He was ready to compromise and so was Indra.

"Let Trishanku, happy as a god, remain suspended where he is. The stars you have created will circumambulate him." Indra said.

Thus Trishanku became the center of the new galaxy with twenty-seven lunar mansions. The seven constellations that Vishvamitra had created would circle him. Trishanku understood that he could not enjoy anything in his *chandala* form, so he agreed to become a star, shining in the sky. At last he was shining for all to see.

As the story unfolded, Vishvamitra was gladdened by Rama's and Lakshmana's responsive smiles and outbursts of laughter. Dusk turned into a star-studded night as Vishvamitra came to the end of the tale.

"See?" he said, pointing at a particularly bright star. "That is my friend, Trishanku." He chuckled lightly and gazed at Rama's lovely face. Lord Vishnu must have been pleased with him somehow, he thought. Otherwise he would not be sitting here in front of the Lord as his teacher. It was a hugely puzzling phenomenon. To sit face to face with God in his human form was a mysterious miracle—the Lord and master of all things sitting quietly, so seemingly unaware of himself. How was it that Rama, though exceptionally attractive, passed for a mere human in others' eyes? It was hard to believe. Yet Vishvamitra's soaring heart told him it was so.

"Thank you for the story," Rama said with a smile.

Vishvamitra's heart melted on hearing Rama's melodious voice. He knew that ultimately Vasishta was more favored in the Lord's eyes, since he had the good fortune of being the family priest and had overseen every step of Rama's development from childhood to adolescence. But Vishvamitra knew that he too had a role to play in the Lord's pastimes, something Vasishta could not do. Originally a Kshatriya, he had extensive knowledge of all the weapons known to both men and gods. Next to Parashuram, the notorious Kshatriya-hater, Vishvamitra was the only person to possess this knowledge. Now he would pass it on to Rama.

"My dear Prince Rama, you have passed my first test with excellence. Please rest well tonight, for tomorrow morning I will pass on to you my knowledge of all weapons, a rare thing to possess. Now sleep."

Rama looked towards Lakshmana as Vishvamitra spoke. Vishvamitra understood at once and agreed that Rama could share this exclusive knowledge with Lakshmana. Both youths beamed. The trio lay down to sleep on the ground, gazing up at the starry blackness. Thrilled by their adventure, neither youth could sleep, despite Vishvamitra's urging. Rama had felt torn while leaving his father, but the feeling had long since vanished. Now he wondered whether his father also lay sleepless this night. Rama and Lakshmana whispered to one another, comparing experiences, until at last sleep overtook them.

Protecting Vishvamitra's Sacrifice

THE NEXT MORNING they rose before the sun did and, clad only in loincloths, dipped into the chilly water of the Ganga. Soon the sun's morning rays dried their skin. Rama and Lakshmana looked expectantly at the noble rishi. Without delay, Vishvamitra took water from his vessel and poured it through his palm onto Rama's hand. They sat in front of the sage, attentively listening. Vishvamitra began by passing on the mantras for the celestial *astras,* the projectile missiles. Rama received *astras* for attack and the knowledge of how to retract or deflect an *astra.* Each weapon's mantra had to be memorized. When spoken aloud, the presiding deity of each weapon appeared before young Rama and acknowledged him as new master.

"What is your command, Master?"

"When I think of you, appear in my hand."

Thus, the entire range of earthly and celestial weapons came into Rama's possession through a true master. Rama, in turn, helped Lakshmana memorize the mantras, making him also the master of the weapons.

"Now you will be able to face anyone in battle and know that you possess the greater knowledge of weaponry," Vishvamitra assured them.

"Let us proceed to my ashram where you will get your first chance to test these weapons. Marichi and Subahu, the two Rakshasa leaders, will be easy targets for you."

The three continued on their journey through greener forests and eventually arrived at Vishvamitra's hermitage where all was ready for the sacrifice to continue. The other hermits came out to greet Vishvamitra and the youths. The ascetics present were minimally clad in loincloths. The austere life they led was evident by the absence of fat on their bodies. The sacrifice began.

Rama and Lakshmana took their bows in one hand and arrows in the other. They circled the area like two sleek panthers on the prowl. Vishvamitra sat in the middle of the arena in front of the fire pit pouring ghee into the fire; the yellow liquid fed the flames. He stared into the fire as the sages around him chanted the mantras in sonorous tones. Vishvamitra's lips were now sealed in a vow of silence.

Nothing interfered with the sacrifice that day or for several thereafter. Six days passed with no sign of disturbance. The sacrifice was blazing gloriously, and mantras poured out along with ladle upon ladle of clarified butter. Rama and Lakshmana, who took the business of protection seriously, remained on constant alert, but the sky was clouded only by smoke from the fire pit. No demons were sighted. On the sixth day, the sacrifice was drawing to a close.

It was then that the cunning demons made their presence known through cackling laughter and cracking noises, louder than thunder. Blood, pus, stool, and urine began raining down on the arena. The only sign the sages showed of acknowledging that they were under attack was to chant louder.

"Lakshmana, beware!" Rama called out, as he placed his first arrow against the bow.

Rama was quick with his bow, and his arrows flew in circles above the sacrificial arena, creating a roof and thus protecting the arena from the offensive liquids. Seeing that their downpour of substances had failed, Marichi and Subahu bared their fangs and prepared to pounce on Rama and Lakshmana. Their flaming red hair whirled through the air as they descended from the clouds. Rama's first arrow hit Marichi with immense force, and he was flung away eight hundred miles, dropping into the middle of the ocean. Rama's second arrow pierced Subahu's chest, hurling him away from the sacrificial floor, pinning him to the ground, and killing him. Their compatriots screamed and tried to escape, but they were caught by the princes' arrows, their heads cut off in mid-air and flung away. Bow and arrow still in hand, Rama and Lakshmana ran around, quickly scanning the arena to make sure no demons had escaped.

Soon after, the sacrifice was completed. Vishvamitra was very pleased with Rama and Lakshmana's capable handling of the ferocious demons. His first words, after a six-day silence, were, "Well done!" He embraced them fondly.

"Now it is time for us to return home. Your father will become worried if I do not return you within the ten days I promised him. But I propose we take a detour through Mithila, King Janaka's city, for he is doing a sacrifice there and has requested all to attend. We will join a caravan of sages who are going there, unless you have an objection?"

"Whatever you decide, we shall do," Rama answered amiably.

Vishvamitra's real purpose in bringing Rama to Mitthila was to show him the great bow in King Janaka's possession. Rumors and stories had long been circulating about the bow as well as about the king's beautiful daughter, Sita. There was also another reason for the detour—an ancient prophesy that Vishvamitra intended to investigate.

The sages joined a caravan of about one hundred carts loaded with the necessary items for the king's sacrifice. Rama and Lakshmana sat in one of the carts with Vishvamitra, talking in a friendly and relaxed manner. They were eager to learn more from him, so they asked him about the history of all the places through which they were traveling. They thus reached Mitthila in high spirits.

A Woman of Stone

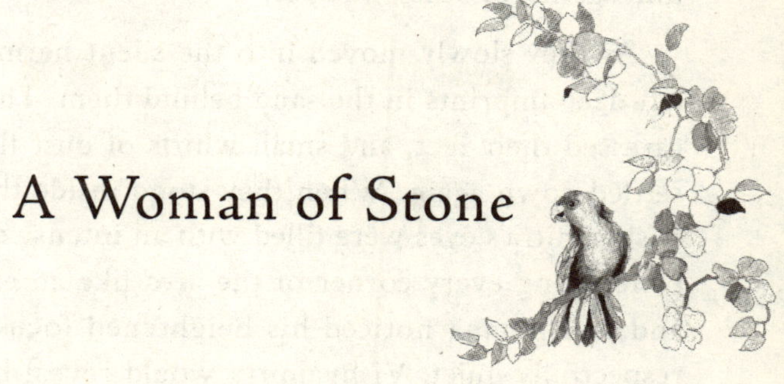

WHEN THE CARAVAN was close enough to Mitthila to see the many flags on the high towers, there was a general commotion among the sages. What a wonderful city! They were happy to have arrived. Invigorated, Vishvamitra climbed out of the cart followed by the two princes. They proceeded on foot, the boys familiarly falling into place behind Vishvamitra.

The dazzling city disappeared from their view as Vishvamitra swerved off the main path to one that was narrow and overgrown with weeds and bushes.

"A shortcut," Lakshmana whispered to Rama.

Rama shrugged but smiled at his brother. Vishvamitra led them forward purposefully. Eventually the neglected path brought them to an empty hermitage. It was ancient and surprisingly empty considering its proximity to the city. The deserted dwelling was filled with a profound silence;

every word and gesture seemed amplified. Responding to this, Rama lightly tapped Lakshmana's hand, cautioning him against another whisper.

As they slowly moved into the silent hermitage, they left deep imprints in the sand behind them. The soft sand caressed their feet, and small whirls of dust flew up and settled down again. When they stood inside the clearing, Vishvamitra's eyes were filled with an intense expectancy, penetrating every corner of the area like an eagle. Rama and Lakshmana noticed his heightened focus and were respectfully quiet. Vishvamitra would reveal his mind at the appropriate time.

The most noticeable feature in the clearing was a shiny black rock, polished by time. The brothers noticed the rock, but did not linger on it. Vishvamitra, on the other hand, focused his eyes intently on the stone. Something hidden from the eyes of mankind since time immemorial was concealed inside. But Vishvamitra had come to discover it, as the ancient prophesy had foretold: "The king-turned-sage Vishvamitra will come bringing with him the pure prince of Ayodhya."

He turned to Rama with gravity. He was about to breach a topic unfamiliar to a child— marriage vows betrayed. However, Rama was on the brink of manhood and must know that dissension and human anguish were facts of life. Up until then their exposure to male-female relationships was mostly limited to their mothers' interaction with their father. To keep such innocence intact was not wise, not in one who was to be king of the world.

Signaling them to come closer to him, Vishvamitra began. "Rama, Lakshmana, all sins committed do not have an immediate retribution. The punishment comes, but the laws of nature are not always clearly discernible. However, I have brought you to this place to talk to you of a human sin committed by two people and the lightning swift punishment that was meted out to them."

His eyes wandered from them back to the rock. "This was once the ashram of the virtuous Gautama and his wife, Ahalya. They lived here performing austerities and purifying their lives. Bound by the vows of marriage, they prospered together. However, Indra, king of the gods, became smitten by the lovely Ahalya. Even though she was the wife of Gautama, he started thinking of ways that he might enjoy her.

"One day when Gautama went for his daily bath, Indra seized his chance. He took the form and dress of Gautama himself and approached Ahalya. Speaking sweetly to her, and praising her appearance, he made his intention clear. She yielded to his advance, forgetting all chastity and loyalty; she enjoyed with Indra as on a first wedding night, though she knew at once that he was not her husband.

"After the union, Indra became nervous and hurried out of the ashram to avoid Gautama. He did not escape unnoticed. Gautama, wet from his bath and pure from his austerity, came face to face with Indra still disguised as Gautama—one rich in virtue and the other with none. Indra immediately felt the full weight of his shameful act and turned ashen in color. When Gautama saw them both stricken with shame before him, his fury knew no bounds.

"His anger took shape in words, which he hurled like a weapon at Indra, 'May you be covered by the private parts of a thousand women!'

"Instantly, Indra's skin was transmuted.

"To his mortified wife, Gautama said, 'You heartless woman, become a stone!' At once her body became rigid and turned into a solid rock."

While he told the story, Vishvamitra's eyes had not moved from the black stone before them. When it dawned on them that this was that very stone, Lakshmana gasped while Rama's eyes widened in disbelief. They looked at Vishvamitra for confirmation.

"Yes. This is that stone. Inside it, Ahalya's being has been trapped. Indra was not punished in the same way but became a laughingstock to the world, his whole body proof of his decadence. It was impossible to conceal or misunderstand the nature of his transgression. Ahalya, at least, suffered her humiliation in privacy. Of course, this incident occurred a very long time ago."

"But how long must she suffer trapped in this stone?" Rama asked, moving nearer to the stone.

"Gautama was a sage with great insight into the future. After he overcame his anger, he agreed that Indra instead be covered by a thousand eyes. And Ahalya would be redeemed, he acquiesced, by the prince of Ayodhya, Ramachandra."

Now Vishvamitra's gaze was on Rama, and Rama finally understood the cause of Vishavmitra's intensity. Rama stared back at the sage, astonished.

"They knew that we would be born and come here?" Lakshmana asked, his eyebrows nearly touching his hairline in incredulity.

Vishvamitra could only shake his head. He too was perplexed. The pattern of birth and death and the ultimate destination for all souls had been set at the inception of the universe, yet because each soul had freedom to choose otherwise at any moment, the accuracy of the prediction was astonishing.

Rama was by that time more concerned for Ahalya, the woman whose one-time transgression had fixed her inside a stone, an eternity of immobility and loneliness touched only by the unrelenting hands of nature, wind, and rain. Rama's attention fixated on the rock, and he softly approached it. What his part was in her salvation, he did not know. It was his compassion that made him approach the woman of stone. As he did, the sand flew up in whirls from his feet and wafted onto the stone. As the dust particles settled down on it, something started melting inside the hard rock.

Emerging from her pall of darkness, Ahalya was awakened by the dust from Rama's feet. Like a lost soul breaking through bondage and transforming the material carcass for the eternal body, Ahalya reached out to the Lord's feet. The rigid stone gave way to a softer element, and Ahalya regained her form and vitality. Curled at Rama's feet, her heart melted.

The ecstasy of relief pervaded her, and with warm tears of reverence, she pressed her forehead to his feet. Rama felt a deep compassion fill his entire being. She had suffered so long. He forgave not only her but each soul like her. Instinctively, he took her by the shoulders and raised her up, his feelings of forgiveness and love transmitting through his hands. The rays of love reached her heart, melting away the last strands of shame and self-recrimination. Because he forgave her, she could free herself from any self-reproach. She had more than atoned for her crime. She basked in the pure glow of her salvation.

At that moment, Gautama, the disgraced husband, mystically appeared. He had come for his wife. She bowed at his feet before he could stop her. After an eternity of separation, he welcomed her back to her rightful place beside him. A sense of great satisfaction filled the air, and then Rama bowed down at the feet of the timeless sage. Vishvamitra and Laksham, who had witnessed the miracle in stillness, came forth to offer their respect. After accepting their obeisance, Gautama and Ahalya disappeared.

The place that Ahalya had occupied was now completely empty. The entire episode seemed like a dream.The trio left the deserted hermitage, leaving only their impermanent footprints behind.

With the two timeless beings gone, and the eerie feeling slowly fading, the need for words arose. With the help of Vishavmitra, the princes tried to put the episode into perspective. Lakshmana was full of questions, and Vishvamitra took pleasure in answering them for he had felt momentarily overwhelmed himself.

Rama was more quiet and full of thought. The feelings he experienced when he had released Ahalya reverberated within him. He could not explain where they had come from or how they had melted the stone, but the power of those feelings was so great that he had been unable to contain it within his physical frame. They emanated from him, embracing the anguished Ahalya and soothing her. Rama felt that each soul in the world was as near and dear to him as his own mother, brother, and father. If he, as his name suggested, was capable of pleasing by his presence alone, his capacity to take action and absolve any given person was far vaster.

Like one who has found the answer to an impossible riddle, Vishvamitra was greatly satisfied by what he had observed. Rama's heart was divided into two equal parts. The steely resolve when he killed Tataka was balanced by a loving compassionate nature, which drew him naturally to protect the weak and redeem the suffering. He could see that Rama himself was overwhelmed.

"Dear prince, when you battled with Tataka, I saw the power of your hands. You have shown that you can kill when necessary, destroying evil. The uncompromising steel of a warrior was manifested. The power to destroy, however, is ruthless. Destroying in itself is an incomplete act if you cannot also absolve and protect. Today, Rama,

you have shown me and yourself that you are a protector. Spontaneously, you were drawn towards Ahalya's suffering, and you released her with a compassion so strong it went through the solid rock."

Rama began to realize his own empowerment.

Vishvamitra addressed further questions from both Rama and Lakshmana, and when all three felt satisifed, they resumed their journey. Coming back onto the main path, the two princes and their guide fell silent as they made their way to the city. A solemn mood settled on them as they entered Mitthila's city gate.

The Bow and the Princess

IN THE CENTER of Mitthila lay a massive bow, waiting. It was an heirloom that had been in King Janaka's family for generations. Legend had it that the bow had originally belonged to Lord Shiva, the lord of dissolution, who had killed three flying demons with it to save the world. Because the bow was so massive in its proportions, few people disputed this legend. No man had ever been known to be able to even lift the bow, let alone string or shoot with it.

King Janaka had publicly declared that only the man who could lift the bow and string it would be allowed to marry his daughter, Sita. Was the king then intent on making a spinster of his lovely daughter?

Many princes had come from afar, yet there the bow lay, unmovable and still waiting. Sita would never marry, it seemed. King Janaka had thought long and hard over his declaration, for Sita had come as a miracle to him; she was born of no mother. How could he give her away in marriage to one of a lesser pedigree? While he didn't repent his declaration, Janaka wondered about the weakness of the current human breed and what would become of Sita if time passed and the bow remained where it was.

Coming into the city, Rama and Lakshmana were wide-eyed with curiosity. This was the first city they had been to other than their own, Ayodhya. Mitthila was beautiful, and the people in it were happy. On one side of the path, Lakshmana saw a clear pond full of blue, red, and white lotuses swarming with bees. On the other side of the path, Rama saw a garden grove full of trees laden with fruits. Colorful flower petals were scattered everywhere on the ground. The garden was also full of young girls, whose cheeks were red from laughing, running, and playing among the trees and bushes. Pure at heart as they were, Rama and Lakshmana appreciated the beauty of both the scenery and the frolicking girls. However, there was hardly time to take in all the city's wonders as they continued to march forward at their usual pace behind Vishvamitra. They had a sacrifice to attend.

After the solemnity surrounding the release of the stone-woman Ahalya, Rama was happy to be enjoying himself in the merry city atmosphere, and he allowed his gaze to wander freely as he walked. Impossible to miss was a large palace full of arched windows and terraces with cushioned swings. Rama saw someone standing on the largest terrace and looking out into the city. The sight of her stunned him and took his breath away. He had never felt the need to look twice at another woman, but he couldn't stop looking at the captivating form of this girl.

She was a miracle of creation. Every woman has a particular beauty, but this girl was a composite of all the beautiful aspects possible in a woman. She was slender and graceful with dainty feminine curves, a tapering waist, full hips, and full round breasts. She looked like a lotus about to bloom. The breeze made the curls of her hair caress her cheeks, and her long black hair lay in waves around her shoulders and hips. Rama's heart was lost in her splendor, and it seemed to him that everyone was staring at her like he was. If Lord Brahma, the creator, was asked to create another like her, he would have to say no, for he had used all his tricks in making this girl. Celestial damsels like Menaka and Urvasi, themselves paragons of beauty and the inspiration of poets, would bow their heads in shame on seeing such stirring loveliness as this girl possessed. Her hands were dainty and delicate, her pinkish palms resting gracefully on the terrace railing. Her eyes were unbelievably large and deep, sparkling, and exquisite with their thick eyelashes curling up and framing their almond outline. Her mouth was as red and full as a ripe berry, and a small, ethereal smile played on her lips, making the beholder eager to know why she was smiling. Her skin was so fair that one would be afraid to touch her, and the rosy blush on her cheeks resembled the color of sunset through a pure white cloud.

She was still, her hand placed over her heart, and Rama saw why when he looked into her eyes. She was staring at him. She was a perfect statue, her breath suspended, and Rama saw his own emotions reflected in her eyes. A profound longing cried out to him from the deep black of her eyes, and Rama felt his eyes were crying out the same longing to her.

Within moments he lost sight of her, as they continued to advance, but for the rest of the day and that night, he saw her again and again in his mind and wondered at her beauty and who she was. He had left his heart with her, and he felt incomplete and agitated in body and mind for the first time in his life. That the girl was Sita he could not know. It was a rare coincidence that the two had even seen each other because Sita resided mostly in the secluded inner chambers of the palace. Few had the good fortune of seeing her, although everyone knew about her miraculous beauty. Musing upon her while attending the fire sacrifice and spending a sleepless night doing the same, Rama arose the next morning, at Vishvamitra's bidding and went off to see the famous bow.

King Janaka was a kind-hearted and peaceful man, so he didn't react when Vishvamitra asked to see the famous bow, although his reason for wanting to see the bow was clear enough with two eligible boys standing behind him. He did shoot a glance or two at Rama's slender arms. On the other hand, he had seen the most muscular arms fail to lift the bow even a millimeter, and he had discovered long ago that the Lord worked in mysterious ways. However unlikely it seemed, maybe Rama would be the one to succeed. If love at first sight was possible between a man and a boy, then Janaka fell instantly in love with Rama. The boy was a natural leader, and the king had never seen one so well-suited to his daughter.

However, he thought that failure was almost a certainty. "These boys are very young." The implication that they were not strong enough for the task hung in the air.

Vishvamitra saw both the king's hesitancy and his willingness to be won over. Therefore, with a few well-chosen words, Vishvamitra outlined Rama's character and attributes. There was no need to emphasize that he was the emperor's son, for King Janaka was not one to judge a man by his social status or his wealth. The succinct praise gladdened Rama because it revealed the force of the older man's affection for him.

"There is more to Rama than meets the eye," Vishvamitra concluded. "Much more."

Vishvamitra knew this was an understatement, but his words seemed right and they fanned the hope that flickered in King Janaka's eyes.

"Well, he certainly is qualified. If Rama can lift the bow, I will, as promised, give him my daughter's hand in marriage."

On his way to Mitthila, Rama had heard the legend of the bow and about the stunning princess who would be won by stringing it. It was an appealing competition for any warrior, since it was a difficult task with an exceptional reward. Rama had not personally desired the princess or wished for the chance to try his luck with the bow. He had been a passive traveler on this trip to Mitthila. Still, he trusted Vishvamitra, so he remained silent when King Janaka escorted them to the bow.

It had been a long time since the king had gone to the hall that held the bow. It had become a bitter disappointment to see the constant flow of people streaming in and out. King Janaka had presided over every trial, seeing prince after prince fail. Now he seldom went, and no one attempted the task either, since it was clear it could not be done. Inside the magnificent hall the bow lay and would remain there until Sita died, or so the crueler people thought.

When King Janaka entered, he was surprised to see the hall crowded with people. Rama and Lakshmana had evidently been noticed as they had made their way through the streets. My people know something, King Janaka thought. They had guessed that one or both of the boys would try, and they wouldn't miss their attempt. It had been a long time now since the last trial, and these boys caused quite a stir, especially the older one, greenish in hue, who resembled a god.

King Janaka led the three to the center and indicated the bow with his hands. Then he stepped back to see what either of them would do. He had seen some men run off after seeing the bow without even trying to lift it; it was a daunting sight. It shone, almost vibrated, and was mounted inside a large case with wheels. Beside it stood a phalanx of tall, well-muscled men. There were, in fact, five hundred bodyguards of the bow. They were responsible for dragging the bow into the hall during the day and removing it at night. It took every muscle of all five hundred men to propel the bow.

Customs, such as deep respect for elders and the idea

that the eldest son marries first, were unquestioned in Rama and Lakshmana's culture. Therefore, Lakshmana did no more than look at the bow from top to bottom and utter an enthusiastic exclamation.

After his inspection, Lakshmana stepped back as Rama stepped forward. Rama was eager to examine the bow; Lakshmana's exclamation could not adequately express his own awakening feelings. Rama's hands went out to touch the dark wood and to feel the heavy fiber. Even at the narrowing ends, the circumference of the ancient bow was greater than Rama's upper arm. He reached out and stroked the smooth surface and knew that he could lift it. The bow was alive; Rama could feel it as a distinct presence.

He turned to Vishvamitra who encouraged him. "Yes, go on. Try your luck."

King Janaka also nodded his consent.

Rama bent down and touched Vishvamitra's feet and broke the solemn moment only when he smiled at Lakshmana. This was like one of their games, similar to an obstacle course, but it was actually the first time that Rama was doing something without Lakshmana. Until that moment, they had reached all their landmarks of growth together. Only Rama was moving ahead now, into that sphere that made him absolutely a man, responsible for a wife.

Rama walked slowly around the bow. The people watched his every move. No one spoke. King Janaka noticed at once the difference between this boy and the others who had come before him. Rama was in no hurry. Many, in their eagerness to prove themselves, immediately clamped their hands on the bow and tried to jerk it up, as if they were champion weightlifters. However, this youth was letting his hands glide across the wood and under it, holding it, but not lifting it. He seemed to be studying it. Rama circled a few times in this manner, feeling the bow. Finally he stopped in the middle where he would be able to put his hands on each side equally. He brought his hands together, maybe to rub them, Janaka thought, as he had seen others do. However, Rama closed his eyes and was praying, hands palm to palm. This boy was different. He went about the procedure in an entirely different manner, and King Janaka's hopes grew. Maybe his daughter would finally find a match. As King Janaka looked at Rama in the center of the hall, he could not help but observe that Rama was equal in beauty to his daughter.

Rama, who stood in silent supplication with his eyes closed, was seeing something through the darkness of his eyelids. A face appeared before him; it was the former owner of the bow. He was dark-skinned and effulgent.

"I do not mean to harm the bow," Rama murmured. "I will lift it, string it, and put it back. I will revere it as if it were my father's."

When Rama opened his eyes, he realized it must have been Lord Shiva, the last one to lift the bow. He had guarded it ever since, not wishing anyone unworthy to use it. Rama's heart was pure and his intention clear. Rama had seen a brief smile on Lord Shiva's face before the vision disappeared.

It was only then that he opened his eyes, for the smile had reassured him that the bow would be conquered.

Now seeing the bow with this knowledge, he noticed a change in its physical structure. It did not shine so brightly. Rather, it had begun to look like a normal bow, though unusually large. The presence that had infused the bow with so much power was gone.

Rama quickly took action. His hand slid under the bow and lifted it up in one swift motion. Anyone slightly inattentive would have missed the feat. Everyone gasped, even Vishvamitra and Lakshmana, who knew Rama could do anything. Vishvamitra was a believer due to his knowledge of Rama's supernatural nature and Lakshmana due to his complete and blind brotherly love. King Janaka would have rubbed his eyes in disbelief, but he was so shocked he could not move.

Rama, meanwhile, was as calm as ever. He stood the bow upright, leaning one tip on the floor. Putting his foot on this tip to steady the bow, he gathered the string into his right hand. The bow was so large he had to stand on his toes to reach the other end of it. The old wood creaked as he shaped it to his will. Slowly it bent, Rama's muscles flexing to bring it into a proper shape. The bow was nearing a perfect arch when suddenly it exploded.

The bow had fulfilled its purpose. The legend of its greatness had been shattered and lay in the pieces of wood scattered on the floor. Now a new legend—how the great bow finally broke—had been created to replace the old one.

The earth almost shook with the explosion, or so it seemed to the people in attendance. Rama grinned, and the next moment everyone was clapping tumultuously and cheering. Lakshmana ran and threw his arms around Rama.

King Janaka nodded his head while tears spurted from his eyes. He could not believe what he had just seen. He couldn't have made a better choice of a husband for Sita himself, but the bow had made this choice for him. The king had been right after all in decreeing that stringing the bow would be the test to find a suitable match for his daughter. This was how his people would talk amongst themselves when Sita was married and gone to her husband's kingdom.

"Bring Sita!" King Janaka called joyfully to his servants. "Adorn her as befits a princess and let her come with a garland in hand."

Sita was lying on her bed like a wilting creeper. She was distracted and feverish. Her maids and surrogate mothers were at a loss. They had never seen her like this. She had spent a sleepless night on the terrace yearning for the handsome bowman she had seen walk away earlier in the day. The soles of his feet were pinkish, and they had looked so soft she was worried they would become bruised from walking barefoot. She had stared at him without shame. He was the embodiment of masculine beauty, and she was shocked at her audacity. She was born with a natural bashfulness and felt shy even with her father.

"Have I lost all sense of decorum?" she wondered. In truth, she didn't care; her mind was overwhelmed with pictures of that bowman and the way he had looked up at her. "Will I ever see him again?" she wondered, despondent.

She did not want to eat or drink and sat quietly looking out into the distance, sometimes leaping up in agitation and running out to the terrace in case he was passing. She was so lost in thought that she didn't hear the loud boom that shook the palace.

Suddenly her maid danced into the room, clapping her hands, spinning and laughing. "You will not believe what has just happened! The bow has been lifted and broken! You are going to be married!"

This awoke Sita from her trance instantly. Was it her bowman? Was it that dark youth from yesterday who had lifted the bow and won her? She blushed deeply with happiness, the mere possibility of it being true filling her with bliss.

"Your father has ordered us to decorate you and bring you to the great hall."

With a mounting sense of urgency, Sita sat down by the mirror and let her maidservants do as they pleased. They sprinkled fragrant flowers in her hair and tied it into a braid, making it look like the night sky, black with white stars. They put sparkling jewels in her ears and matching gems around her neck and hips. Many fresh flower garlands were tied into her hair and around her wrists. The ankle bells tinkled when they put them around her lotus feet. Their efforts were not necessary, for could Sita possibly be made more beautiful?

Then, placing a black mark on the side of her chin to symbolically mar her perfection and thus ward off evil or envious eyes, they lifted her and led her down to the hall.

Sita went, praying and hoping that she would see that

slender, green-hued bowman in the hall. She took only shallow breaths, and she glowed like the full moon. As they entered the hall, Sita could hear the pleased cheering and joyous noises. She was afraid to look up and see the man standing in the middle with the broken bow around him. What if it wasn't him? She trembled. She was careful to keep her eyes downcast. When she came closer, she was able to see his feet. She had to control her lips, which wanted to curve into a smile. Those were the same feet she had seen the day before. Her inner voice sang songs of love, warming her heart. Her happiness in those moments was so deep that she didn't know what to do with her eyes, which darted here and there like black bumblebees.

After breaking the bow, Rama was poised but his heart beat in unison with the enthused claps of the people around him. His heart hadn't regained its normal pace when he realized they were bringing Sita to him. He was stunned when he saw it was the girl from the terrace, the girl he had dreamed of. How his heart started beating then only a lover can imagine. However, no one can imagine the depth of emotion that passed between the two, because it was not just two lovers uniting. On a deeper level, Sita and Rama, the divine companions, were being reunited. Sita and Rama were the eternal Lakshmi and Vishnu, although they themselves did not remember it.

Although Lakshmana was standing near him, Rama's mind took a leap away from boyhood, leaving Lakshmana behind. He lost all trace of boyishness in those moments when he stood waiting for Sita to approach, waiting for her to see him and to garland him as her lord. His heart was already hers, his loyalty from then on divided between Sita and his brother.

King Janaka led his blushing daughter forward, accompanied by all her jubilant friends. When she stood in front of Rama, drops of perspiration lined the arches of her eyebrows, and her eyelashes held small tears. Slowly she looked up into his face. After that she looked nowhere else. Her eyelids fluttered, and the tears rolled down from her eyes. The delicate fingers holding the garland trembled slightly. Whatever emotion was swirling in her she saw mirrored in him. King Janaka put one hand on Rama's shoulder; the other was already resting on Sita's.

"Rama, son of our emperor King Dasharatha, will you accept my daughter Sita as your wife?"

"Yes," Rama answered without looking away from her.

"Sita, put the garland on him if you also consent to this marriage."

The king spoke the required formal words, but there was no formality in his tone. Sita lifted the flower garland and placed it on Rama's neck as he bent down so she could reach. They smiled at each other shyly. Flower petals showered them from every direction, and the cheering grew louder as the news of the betrothal spread. The bow was broken and their princess would marry!

A messenger was immediately sent to a surprised King Dasharatha. Meanwhile, the two lovers spent a few days

shyly gazing at each other and exchanging sweet words until the king reached the gate of Mitthila with his accompanying party. There was much to celebrate when King Dasharatha arrived, and the people were jubilant. King Dasharatha, who would have been more than satisfied simply to see Rama again, now happily welcomed Sita into his family. They were a beautiful, well-matched couple.

When the two fathers sat down with their advisors and royal preceptors to discuss the wedding formalities and preparations, King Dasharatha surprised King Janaka with a request: "Rama is already entitled to Sita's hand because he passed the test that you set. However, I humbly request the hand of your second daughter, Urmila, for my son Lakshmana."

"O King, I agree to your proposal without objection. I agree wholeheartedly!"

Vasishta and Vishvamitra then additionally requested that the two daughters of Kushadvaja, Janaka's younger brother, be given in marriage to Bharata and Shatrugna. There was a unanimous agreement on all sides, and thus the quadruple marriage was decided upon and fixed for three days later, during an auspicious hour known as *vijay*, "victory."

On their wedding day, the four princes were bathed by their mothers and smeared with sandalwood mixed with saffron. They were clad in the finest of silks, and flower garlands hung to their knees. They were brought to the sacrificial arena and settled down to wait for their princesses to arrive. In her wedding attire, Sita came to Rama looking more magnificent than a goddess. Urmila sat by Lakshmana, both of them bashful and expectant. Simultaneously, Mandavi was led to Bharata and Shrutakirti to Shatrugna.

Standing by Rama's side, King Janaka took Sita's hand in his own and, with a voice trembling with emotion, addressed

Rama. "This is my daughter Sita. Please take her hand and accept her as your life's partner. She possesses all good qualities and will forever be devoted to you. She will follow you as closely as your own shadow."

He placed Sita's fair hand into Rama's dark one, and their union was thus sealed. Rama felt great satisfaction at having won Sita as his wife. King Janaka then placed the hands of his other daughter and his two nieces in the hands of their respective grooms. Fires were lit, vows exchanged, and the four pairs circumambulated the fire and then their elders. Amid great celebration, the newlyweds retired for the night.

The next morning, both Sita and Rama faced tearful farewells. Sita had to leave her father, a distress not lessened by the knowledge that all girls went through the same separation. Rama, meanwhile, had to bid Vishvamitra good-bye. Their association had lasted barely ten days, but they had been the most tumultuous and enlivening days of Rama's life so far. He regretted to see Vishvamitra leave. Rama and Lakshmana said what they could to express their deep gratitude and respect, touched Vishvamitra's feet, and watched him depart to the Himalayas, the great mountain peaks of the north.

The journey home started with pleasure because each princess had found her prince and was satisfied with him.

The Newlyweds Disturbed

WHEN THE TRAVELING party was on the outskirts of Mitthila, birds began to screech, and a fierce wind knocked down several trees around them. Darkness fell, and the party was panic-stricken by the sudden change. Only Dasharatha, Vasishta, and the four brothers were unmoved. Parashuram, the Kshatriya-hater, then strode out of the darkness onto their path, stopping their journey. The breaking of such a great bow could not go unnoticed, and Parashuram had heard the sound of the breaking and could not picture a mortal lifting it. Parashuram hated arrogant Kshatriyas. To punish the crime of one Kshatriya who had beheaded his innocent father, Parashuram had killed twenty-one generations of Kshatriyas, nearly causing the extinction of the race. In his anger he was ready to start the bloodshed again.

"Who among you is the fool who broke Lord Shiva's bow?" he shouted, his eyes bloodshot.

His large battle-ax rested against his muscular shoulder, and on his other brawny shoulder hung a massive bow, a replica of the one Rama had recently broken. Dasharatha felt panic enter his heart.

"Most mighty Parashuram with stone pillars for arms," Dasharatha started, "my son has not purposefully done any wrong. He is not your foe. Is it worthy of someone with your prowess to challenge a boy? Remember your vow to keep peace. Please spare my son. Without him my life and dynasty cannot continue. I place my head on your feet."

Parashuram ignored the king and walked straight to Rama. For some moments, Parashuram was bewildered by Rama. Could this young man really have lifted the bow? Something told him to bow down at Rama's feet or at least to embrace the young man, but his anger predominated.

"Listen to the history of the bow you so irreverently broke," he began. "Vishvakarma, the gods' architect, made two identical matchless bows. Lord Vishnu liked one, and Lord Shiva fancied the other. The gods wondered which of the bows was stronger? Lord Brahma contrived a reason for the two lords to fight. During the fight, Lord Shiva's bow cracked, and Lord Vishnu severed his opponent's bowstring, thus coming out victorious. Shiva gave his bow to Janaka's ancestors, and Lord Vishnu's bow came into my possession through my father. You think you are so powerful! Lord Shiva's bow was already cracked. There is no true merit in having broken a damaged bow. Take Lord Vishnu's bow and fight me if you dare."

Without a word, Rama snatched the huge bow from

Parashuram's hand and effortlessly drew back the string, an arrow in place. Parashuram was shocked. He had never imagined that the boy would have had the strength to even hold the bow, but here he was handling it easily, ready to shoot an arrow.

"Because you are a Brahmin and related to Vishvamitra, to whom I am indebted, I will not kill you," Rama said, the arrow drawn close to his ear. "However, this arrow cannot be placed on the bowstring in vain. I will, therefore, destroy your ascetic merit with this arrow. For challenging me unnecessarily you will have to begin your penance again."

The bow twanged as he shot the arrow into the faraway clouds. Parashuram was humbled and subdued.

This must be Lord Vishnu himself, he thought. Therefore he did not feel ashamed at having been defeated by a Kshatriya and such a young boy at that. Instead, he folded his hands in prayer, accepted his bow from Rama, and left without further comment.

After this obstacle was overcome, the marriage party continued their journey home. Rama's competent handling of Parashuram earned him respect and a new authority, when before he had been considered a child or a youngster.

When they reached Ayodhya, they were greeted joyously by the citizens. Rama and Sita and the other married couples settled in, and years flew by as the young people exchanged sweet words and loving moments.

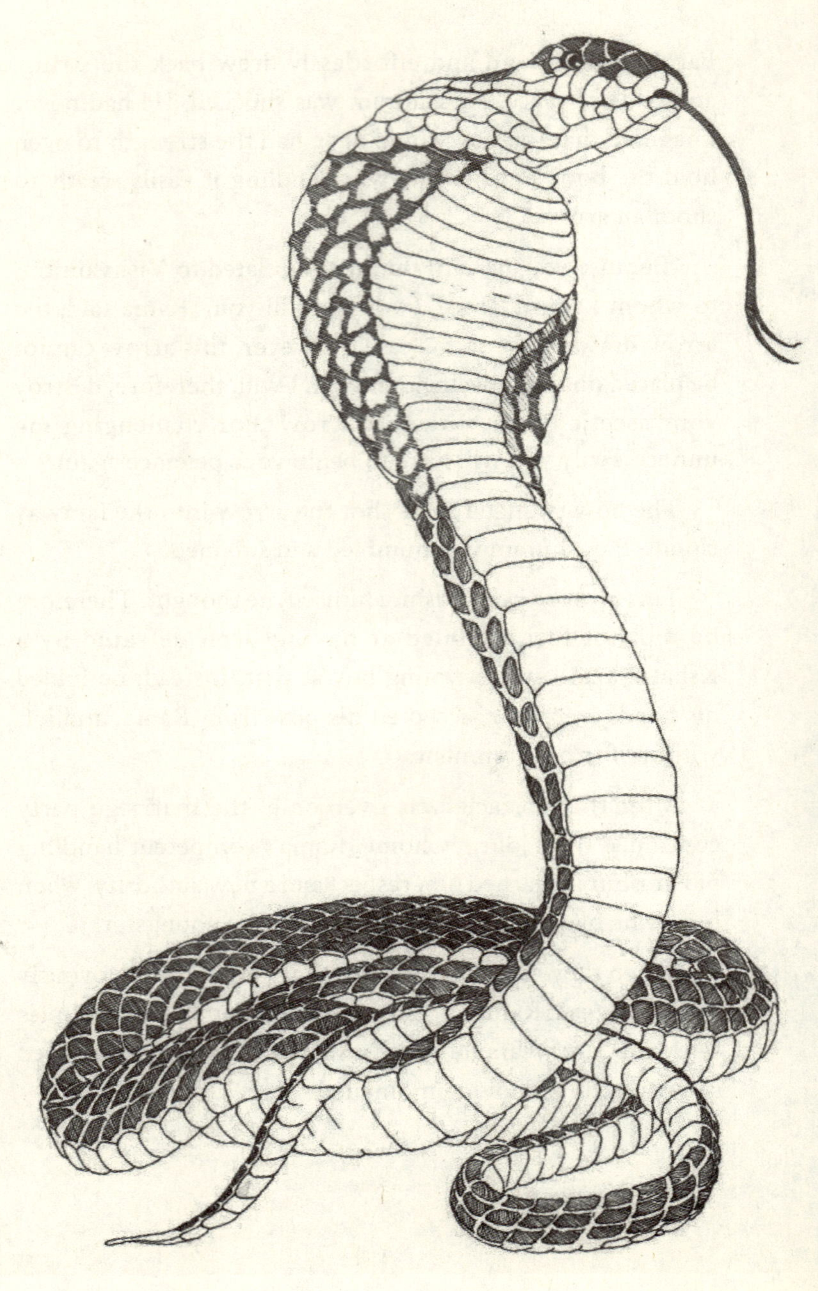

Evil Omens Scare King Dasharatha

KING DASHARATHA STARED into the hypnotic eyes of the swaying snake. Beads of sweat stung his eyes as he tried not to blink. The snake looked ready to strike, and he imagined the sharp fangs penetrating his flesh, its venom mixing with his royal blood. His ability to remain motionless was paramount to his survival. Suddenly the reptile changed tactics and slithered closer, wanting to choke, not bite. The king was paralyzed with fear. He screamed silently, and the snake hissed in his ear while encircling his throat. He gasped for air, for life, and suddenly found himself gazing upward toward a red canopy, silken sheets clinging to his sweaty body. A dream, he realized.

He was perspiring all over. Kaikeyi's thick braid lay heavily across his throat. He sat up and irritably flung it aside. The dream left him with a feeling of imminent disaster that was harder to shake off, but he resisted the urge to quickly leave the bed. Instead, he steadied his mind, telling himself the cobra was an illusion.

Dreaming of a black cobra was a bad omen. This was not the first inauspicious portent he had recently seen, and he began to feel worried. As always, he thought of Rama. What more valuable thing than Rama did he have to lose? He wanted to run to Rama's palace and see his sleeping son. Many times he had done this when Rama was a baby, but now Rama was more than his son; he was a married man. Even the king would feel awkward disturbing Rama and Sita in their private chambers. Although over ten happy years had passed since their marriage, he still considered them hardly more than newlyweds.

"Maybe I'm getting old," he thought, looking at Kaikeyi's tranquil face as she slept. "Bearing the world's burdens belongs to younger shoulders than mine." Vasishta had suggested that stress was a probable cause of the king's anxiety. Yes, it was time for Rama to take over the kingdom. The old king rose from his bed and decided that today he would consult Vasishta on the subject. How would the people feel about a new king?

King Dasharatha summoned the leading citizens of Ayodhya and all the mighty monarchs of the earth. He waited until the large retinue had settled into the court before he addressed them gravely with a resonant voice.

"My dear citizens, you have allowed me to rule you for many years now. I am no longer the vigorous man I was when I became your king. With your permission, I wish to appoint my eldest son Ramachandra as my successor."

The people's immediate shout of happiness soothed the king's worries. But to make sure they were not only trying to please him, he posed a question.

"Why are you so eager to see my son rule in my place? Have I not worked for your welfare and ruled righteously?"

"Your son, dearest king," they replied, "has enhanced the Solar dynasty's glory by his exemplary actions. We believe every word he says because we have seen that he is devoted to truth. He exemplifies nobility by his even-temper, gentle speech, and love for righteousness. We trust his strength because he has never been defeated in battle, and he takes time to reassure us that we are safe. When he returns to the city after being away, he asks after the citizen as if they were members of his own family. He shares in our joy and sorrow as if he were our father. All the citizens remember Rama in their daily prayers. You fulfill our wishes by appointing him as your heir, for we already worship him. Crown him without any delay—that will give us great happiness!"

When the king heard these words, his heart swelled with a joy. Everything was progressing as it should. Dasharatha decided that there was no reason to delay Rama's installation. Bharata and Shatrugna had gone to visit their maternal home but, remembering all the evil omens, the king felt he could not wait for their return. He would install Rama as heir-apparent the very next day.

Annapurna

The Plot

THE PEOPLE WHO had been present in the great hall during the announcement of Rama's installation had now gone home and were spread throughout Ayodhya. Each shared the news with family and friends who had not been present, and everyone was excited. The whole city was energised as the people started preparing gifts for their next king, selecting suitable outfits for the occasion, and talking about their hopes for the future with one another. A few of the palace servants stood on the rooftop and chattered about the great event about to take place. One of these servants was Rama's wet nurse, and next to her stood Manthara, Kaikeyi's old servant. Manthara had come to see what the commotion was all about because the news had not yet reached her. She soon found out everything from the exultant nurse.

A person's outer appearance is certainly not an accurate indicator of his or her nature, but in Manthara's case, it was. Her mind was as crooked as her hunched body. Born with a large hump on her back, she was forced to face the floor rather than the world. Craning her neck up while the rest of her was pulled down by gravity, she would have appeared painfully humble were it not for her facial mien. Her mean eyes revealed her mindset as they darted here and there searching for something to complain about. The clunk of her walking stick was one of the only unpleasant sounds heard in the palace, outdone only by her hoarse, nagging voice. Manthara was a lonely outcast. Although few were rude to her face, she was likely to accuse people randomly of eyeing her hump and gossiping about her. Not surprisingly, she was herself the most fantastic gossiper Ayodhya had ever seen. Possibly because her own misery seemed endless, she derived pleasure from creating misery in the lives of others. She was naturally talented at keeping her ears sharp and her tongue wagging wherever in the palace she hobbled through.

The news about Rama's installation was a dirty enough affair. She barely needed to exaggerate her facts. Full of a gossiper's thrill at having stumbled over an authentic scandal, she headed to Kaikeyi, her mistress and only friend and companion. She thumped her walking stick heavily on the ground and on the feet of people too slow in making way for her. "Out of my way!" she brayed.

Her old hag's face was scrunched up, and her mouth was a tight line of wrinkles. The cogs in her brain turned quickly, and alarming thoughts wound round and round. This news was terrible! Rama to be king? What about Bharata? He would become a second son forever. Kaikeyi's position as favored queen was going to be severely challenged if

Kausalya's son became king. Manthara wasn't stupid enough to believe her antics and sour ways were tolerated out of kindness alone. She knew that Kaikeyi's strong position with the king protected her from direct attack. She enjoyed a superior position to these other common servants. Was she not the most loved servant of the king's most loved wife? It was a position she had taken advantage of, ordering away and even beating whomever she wanted with her cane. She did not want to see what was in store for her if the tables were turned suddenly. Her privileges were endangered, and she had never been fond of Rama in any case, ill-mannered child that he had been in her eyes. Entering Kaikeyi's chamber, she found her mistress reclining on a luxurious throne.

"Kaikeyi! What are you doing on that couch? You might be thrown into the streets at any moment!"

Kaikeyi laughed, but didn't move. "I'm getting my beauty rest."

"Oh, stop it! Save your humor."

"For someone who has humor?"

"Kaikeyi, get up at once and realize the gravity of the situation!" Manthara waved her cane in the air in frustration.

"You forget, my dear, that I have no idea what grave situation you are so wild about, unless you are about to drop that cane on me!"

Kaikeyi's calm was like a wind on Manthara's fire, making her blaze up even more. However, Kaikeyi knew Manthara too well to be infected by her moods when every week had a "grave" situation to be dealt with.

Banging her stick on the floor for emphasis, Manthara again commanded Kaikeyi.

"Get up, I say! Then I'll tell you."

"All right," Kaikeyi said, raising herself slightly. "I'm up."

"Rama is going to be installed as heir apparent to the kingdom tomorrow morning and he will be the next king of Ayodhya," she said in one breath.

"Manthara! That is wonderful news."

Kaikeyi sat up at once.

"Tomorrow. The installation is tomorrow."

"Today, tomorrow—what does it matter? Rama will make a perfect king. I'm so happy to hear this news! No one will rule the kingdom better than my dear Rama."

"'My dear Rama?' What are you saying?"

Kaikeyi, sparkling, got up and unfastened the largest gem she was wearing, presenting it to Manthara.

"This is for bringing me such good news."

"Have you gone mad?" Manthara exclaimed, looking at the large stone in her hand.

"No, have you?" Kaikeyi joked. "Don't feel shy. Keep it. You deserve it!"

"Do you think I care about this tiny jewel? You are the biggest fool on earth!" She threw the gem to the marble floor and glared in defiance at her mistress.

"Manthara!" Kaikeyi's temper flared. She tolerated a lot from Manthara, but not this kind of open insolence. "How dare you behave like this? Get out of my sight at once or I shall really speak words of anger and regret them later."

Undaunted, Manthara screamed back, "I do not care if you are angry at me or if you punish me or beat me, for soon we will both be begging in the streets."

"Manthara, you are talking crazily. What is this madness about?"

"Can't you see? Can't you see that Rama's coronation is the beginning of your downfall as Dasharatha's favorite queen?"

"The king loves all his wives equally," Kaikeyi countered weakly, for the king's favoritism was never spoken of.

"Please do not be modest with me. Play your game with others but not with me. I've known you from your birth, don't forget. You are Dasharatha's favorite queen and you know it."

Kaikeyi blushed happily, and since no one was there to hear it, she said proudly, "So what?"

"So that's all going to change now if Rama becomes king."

"I don't understand at all. Rama is a son to me, and I am truly happy to see him crowned."

"But you are forgetting one detail," Manthara said, spinning her yarn carefully now, knowing she had the queen's attention. Manthara was skilled in speech, and she knew her queen well. She chose words that would bring dejection to Kaikeyi's heart. "Rama is not your son. He is Kausalya's son—the son of your co-wife, who is jealous of you and probably even hates you."

"Yes, but Rama loves me even more than his own mother. He will never let harm befall me."

"You are naïve. Everyone changes when they taste power. Listen to me, Kaikeyi, because your grief is my grief. Only if you prosper can I prosper; there is no doubt in this. I will not mislead you. Now, do you seriously think that Kausalya has no influence over her own son? The balance of power is about to tip toward Kausalya. She will become the most valuable queen in the king's eyes with her son on the throne."

"I somehow feel that you are tying ends together that do not actually meet." Kaikeyi sat down, beginning to feel bewildered. "The king has loved me greatly during these years and so has Rama. Nothing has changed. Rama is virtue incarnate and the most considerate person I have ever known. He loves all of us equally, his mothers and his brothers."

"You are talking like a fool. All this nonsense about feelings and love... I'm talking about practical reality." Manthara sat down close to the queen on the couch. "Kausalya has envied your beauty and youth since you arrived, old prune that she is. She will use this opportunity to root you out. In the past you have disrespected her in your pride. Won't she finally take her revenge? Trust me, you will become her maidservant."

"No!"

"Yes! You and Bharata will become slaves without rights under the rule of Rama and his mother."

"No, Manthara, no. Rama loves us."

"Love again! Is that your best argument? Rama is a learned man in the affairs of state. His actions are timely and appropriate. A king in power must weed out anyone who threatens his throne, and Bharata is next in line among the brothers. He is the only brother who is really in danger because Rama protects Lakshmana and Lakshmana protects Rama. Shatrugna is the youngest. When I think of what will become of Bharata under Rama's rule, I'm overwhelmed with fear."

"If Rama has the kingdom, Bharata has it as well. Rama thinks of his brothers as his own self. Moreover, Rama is fair. No doubt he will rule for a hundred years and then hand over the kingdom to Bharata to rule."

"Such ignorance! It doesn't befit you, daughter of Kekaya. Or are you forgetting, in your fear, that I'm right after all? After Rama rules, his sons will take over. That is the way the dynasty perpetuates itself. Bharata will never get close to the throne—unless he stands behind the throne to fan Rama! Rama is his elder brother by only a few hours. Bharata's life is in danger. Better you advise him to stay in your father's house or send him far, far away. Rama will throw him in the dungeon or kill him. Be sure of that. And you—what Kausalya will do to you, you can imagine."

Kaikeyi shook her head. She did not want to believe a word that her old servant was saying. Her husband, her reason to live, and her sweet Rama loved her very much. They would not harm Bharata. She was sure of it. They would never dismiss her. Or would they? Those words had appeared in her mind without prompting, like two ice-cold insects crawling in where least welcome. Would they?

Seeing the confusion playing on Kaikeyi's face, Manthara made her final insinuation. "If you have any doubts about the king's sincerity..."

"No!" Kaikeyi protested with the kind of passion people use to deny what they don't want to beleive.

"I will give you proof," Manthara said, with evident satisfaction.

"As I first emphasized, tomorrow is the installation." She paused dramatically, "Tomorrow."

"I still do not see the connection."

"Why is your dear king in such haste ?" Manthara paused again, satisfied to see that Kaikeyi was holding her breath. "Because Bharata is not here," she concluded. "The king wants to finish everything before Bharata or your father comes to know of it, before they can stop it. Think, my dear, think! Why an installation all of a sudden? Why can't he wait for Bharata to return? Why didn't he inform you of these proceedings? Even Rama's wet nurse, a mere servant, knows. It was from her that I got the details. And you, the so-called favorite queen, are left in the dark. Is it a coincidence? And your father and Bharata have not even been informed or invited. Why isn't your husband waiting for all the family members to be present for such a momentous occasion? Shouldn't your father be informed that his grandson is being robbed of the throne? Didn't the king promise your father that your son would rule?"

"He thought then that my son would be his only son and thus his eldest," Kaikeyi defended weakly. She was shaken by Manthara's accusations, and she couldn't deny that there was some logic behind them. The king had not mentioned anything to her about his plan to install Rama. He had seemed worried lately. Was it guilt? Had he been afraid she would disapprove? Or worse, was he planning to abandon her in favor of Kausalya, as Manthara was predicting? Her mind agitated by doubt, she turned to Manthara. With every passing moment she began to see why Manthara was so angry and certain of impending doom. Her troubled mind told her she had to do something.

"What should I do? If all this is true... What should I do?"

"It is true! But don't worry, my dear. Manthara has figured it all out. I have a plan."

"Yes, I must do something. I cannot sit by quietly."

"And you will not. You will fight. Listen to me. I will tell you exactly what to do. But first you must promise me to do exactly as I say."

Kaikeyi, completely won over, clutched the old woman's hands. "Yes, I promise. Tell me. I cannot bear this."

Manthara pulled Kaikeyi's head nearer and whispered in her ear. Kaikeyi's face turned from desperate confusion to steely determination. She was going to do as Manthara advised. They had a plan.

Two Old Boons Redeemed

THE DAY QUICKLY became night before Dasharatha halted the preparations for the installation. He then headed straight to Kaikeyi's chambers, as was his habit. His mind buzzed with all the loose ends he had to tie together before tomorrow's event would become the perfect occasion he wanted it to be. Actually, just placing Rama in front of the people and saying, "This is your new king" would be enough. One and all adored Rama, and the citizens would roar their approval. But the formality of installing him as heir-apparent was nevertheless necessary.

When he saw Kaikeyi's palace gate his heartbeat quickened. He laughed aloud when he realized why. What a joy to have a wife like her. He longed to relax in her proximity and to share his exhilaration about the upcoming installation. He was sure the news would delight her. The uneasy thought of his promise from years ago to crown her son was easily crowded out by many memories of Kaikeyi's abundant love for Rama. "I love him so!" she often said.

Her father, Kekaya, might possibly become disgruntled but not Kaikeyi. He hurried into the bedroom. However, she didn't greet him sweetly at the door as she usually did. Maybe she was already asleep, he thought, although he knew she wouldn't go to bed without him.

"Kaikeyi, you won't believe the wonderful news I have to tell you," he said.

The room was empty.

"Kaikeyi," he said a bit louder, "where are you? Hmm..." He murmurred and stroked his beard reflectively. She was always there when he arrived. He looked around the luxurious chamber and heard musical instruments mingling with the sound of parrots and peacocks. The ornate ivory and silver throne-like seats surrounded by creepers and flowers were made for romance. These were things he ordinarily did not notice when Kaikeyi was in front of him. Where was she?

Her absence agitated him significantly. Maybe all the bad omens he had been seeing of late were not about Rama at all, as he had so quickly assumed. Maybe they were about Kaikeyi. A vision of her lying in a pool of blood flashed through his mind. He had been preoccupied with Rama's safety, but his fear for Rama now abated as concern for his other beloved surfaced. His heart pounding with unease, Dasharatha turned away from the desolate chamber and began to search.

To his enormous relief, he found out from a maidservant that the queen had gone to the sulking chamber. Such was the luxury of the palace that a place was set aside where all negative moods were allowed to run their course. In this way the rest of the palace remained an oasis only for pleasant, uplifting emotions. Surely the sulking chambers were not often used, for his queens were all royal and forgiving by nature, but Dasharatha had on occasion been required to go there and settle disputes between his wives or appease some private vexation. As he hurried to the sulking chamber, he wondered if he had forgotten some landmark event again. He had been guilty of that sin before, but he doubted this was the case now, since he had been sufficiently chastened in the past. He searched his mind but could only imagine that his wives must have quarrelled.

Pushing aside the black curtain, he ventured into the dimly lit room. The hall did little to uplift anyone's mood, he thought, as he squinted into the dark corners to find Kaikeyi. He stepped on an earring. He saw that it was one that he had given her last year. He found its match some distance away. Not a good sign, as the distance implied that she must have flung them. She could be like a tempest if displeased. Dasharatha walked on, picking up discarded jewelry—a heavy necklace, a number of precious rings, and anklets. He saw a cascade of bangles and a small heap of flowers on the floor. He followed the trail into a secluded room to the side, his hands now weighed down by the solid gold ornaments that somehow did not look as heavy when they decorated Kaikeyi's lovely limbs.

Taking a few steps into the room he suddenly dropped all that he had carefully picked up. So unprepared was he for the sight of Kaikeyi splayed out on the floor, her black hair scattered, half covering her face and snaking around her neck and arms. Her distress was clear, for she was convulsing with silent sobs, which made her body roll back and forth, arch and go limp. She banged her fists against the floor and shook her head back violently from side to side. Dasharatha stumbled over the gold ornaments and ran to her, his heart in his throat.

"My love, my love!" he exclaimed full of passion and fear. He dropped to his knees and pulled her writhing body into his arms.

She cried, "No!" in a voice hoarse from sobbing, and immediately went limp in his arms. Her head fell back, and her eyes refused to look at him.

His heart was now beating audibly, and as much to calm himself as her, he said, "All is well. I'm here now. I'm here." He stroked her hair again and again and kissed the top of her head. What on earth could have happened?

He continued questioning her while wiping the perspiration from her brow and hugging her tightly. But none of his queries hit the mark, for he was unsuccessful in eliciting a response from her or arousing her to animation. Displaying the depth of his power and to what lengths he'd go to appease her, he asked, "Is there a murderer I shall set free? Or is there an innocent man that I shall execute? I will make a poor man rich, Kaikeyi, or if you like, a rich man poor!"

Still she remained inanimate, and the king was sick with worry, "I swear on Rama, your son, that I will punish. . . "

"Leave me," she interrupted shrilly and rolled out of his startled arms back onto the floor. "Leave, leave, leave!" she cried, then closed her mouth and would say no more.

Dasharatha was dumbstruck. He scarcely recognized her as she stared up at the ceiling as if dead. "Kaikeyi," he said desperately, "what has happened to bring you to this state? I implore you, please, on the strength of the love we share, tell me what ails you." He moved toward her again, but she rolled over several times, creating a clear gap between them. A tear rolled down the king's cheek. "I will not move from here until you speak to me. Speak. Please speak."

A short silence ensued, and he listened to her breathing pattern, which was certainly steadier than his by now. He was about to voice his plea again when she began to speak in an emotionless voice he had never heard her use. "Do you remember when I used to serve on the battlefield as your charioteer?"

"Yes," he replied immediately. "There was none as proud as I was to have a wife not only beautiful but a true warrior-queen, capable in a battle."

A contemptuous laugh escaped from her mouth before she asked, "Do you remember that day when your wounds were so severe you would have expired had I not taken you from the battlefield and stopped your blood flow?"

"Yes," he said quietly. He refrained from saying that he

would never forget that day, for she had saved his life and from then on had been the undisputed object of his love. They had stayed on the outskirts of the battlefield afterwards. He had been too weak to survive being moved back to his palace. She had been like a tigress, fiercely prepared to attack anyone approaching while she simultaneously tended his wounds. After that, it had become hard to stay apart, so intensely had they bonded. His life was hers. Yes, he did remember.

"Do you remember those two boons you offered me?"

"Which you denied, saying you had all that you wished for now that I was alive."

"Yes, and you insisted that I keep them for later," she persisted, still speaking in a monotone. "Now that time has come."

"Is that all, my love?" he said with evident relief, for he was uncertain where this reminiscence was heading. "You did not have to remind me of the past like this. I am ready to give you anything you want."

"Anything?" she asked, with the first quiver of feeling.

He said, solemnly, "On the love I have for my eldest son, Rama, who is the jewel of our dynasty, I promise to give you anything." The words echoed inside him. When had he said these very same words before?

Kaikeyi's face lit up but not in her usual beautiful and loving way. She sat up, unsmiling, and he perceived that there were yet miles to cover before she was reconciled to him.

"I swear on Rama, anything," he repeated.

She stood up then, seeming to think she needed to regain some of her majesty before proceeding. He also stood, and for the first time she faced him squarely.

"King Dasharatha of the Sun dynasty, originating from the sun-god," she began formally. "You come from a line of king's renowned for keeping their word."

"Kaikeyi, what's the need for all this?" He was becoming increasingly worried.

"Do you promise me on the strength of your ancestral line and to redeem your old boons to give me what I ask?"

The king was now perspiring. There can only be one answer to a beloved. His voice shook, but he renewed his promise.

"Do you swear to fulfill my desires twice over?"

"Yes."

"First, I want my son, Bharata, to be installed as king. This is my first wish. Second, let Rama be exiled to the forest for fourteen years to live like a recluse with matted hair, wearing only deerskins."

Dasharatha felt like laughing. Exile Rama? Simultaneously an overwhelming fear and hysteria overcame him. Everything became dim while Rama's beautiful features glowed like a fire before him. Rama, Rama, Rama, echoed in his mind.

He fainted.

The queen's tightly compressed lips formed an "O," and she ran forward to catch him. Her love for the king was too strong to curb her natural reflex. Although she looked completely womanly, she was strong enough to intercept and cushion his fall. However, the hard shell that was now around her heart made her stand up again and move away from him. She refused to feel sympathy for the slumped figure of her husband. If it was true what Manthara had said—that he didn't love her but only loved Rama and that Kausalya would throw her to the dogs the moment her son was king—she couldn't bear it. She took shelter in her early warrior training, thinking only of her goal and never about how many she must kill to achieve it.

Patiently, she sat down to wait for him to recover. If he said her name while coming to, it would be a sign of her victory. She soon fell into a light sleep, lying on the floor, her mind waiting for the first syllables from his mouth.

"Rama," he mumbled half an hour later.

Kaikeyi opened her eyes and knew that no compromise would be possible in this war. The moment consciousness again descended upon him, he sprang up like an arrow and had to steady himself against a pillar for a second.

"Kaikeyi," he tried, but choked on her name.

She raised one eyebrow, questioningly, and said, "Don't tell me you are becoming weak in your old age. I'm just asking you to part with one of your sons. You have three more, although you seem to care little for them by comparison. I'm not asking you to kill Rama, only to send him away until Bharata's rule is established. We could live happily here without him."

His eyes brimmed with tears over Kaikeyi's betrayal of Rama. He heard her words but could not accept their cruel intent. She wanted to separate the eldest and dearest son from his father.

Kaikeyi sat up, the curve of her hip more pronounced as she leaned on one arm. Her thick hair fell over her face so that only one eye looked up at the king. Was she possessed? He went to her slowly and knelt down. He pushed her hair behind her ear and cupped her face gently with both hands.

"My love, my queen, my sweet wife," he began. Tears streamed through his words. "You love Rama. Rama is a tiger among men who advises and cares for all beings with a clear mind. He has captivated each and every one in the kingdom with his kind actions. He is richly endowed with honesty and is as splendorous as a sage. You have said so yourself a million times. You have also said that whatever makes Rama happy makes you happy."

She sat like a stone.

"You always said he was just like your own son."

"Just like. Ha!" She glared at him with manic passion. "He is not my son. I would gladly drink poison before accepting him as a son."

The king's breath left his lungs, and his stomach contracted at the harshness of her words. "Oh, God. Oh, God." He shut his eyes to block the sight of this woman whom he had minutes ago loved more than his life. His hands tightened around her face for a few seconds. His hot breath moistened the curls around her face. She stared at him without blinking. Weakness in a man was something she had never liked. Her heart throbbed wildly and angrily with the knowledge that Rama was so much more to the king than she was.

"If you don't send Rama away now, I will drink poison and kill myself." Her chin quivered. Would he prefer her death to losing Rama?

She fought hard to appear unmoved when Dasharatha shouted, "Good! Kill yourself. I would rather part with all my wives, including you, than part with Rama, my son. My son."

She felt like shouting back but instead whispered, hissing like a cobra, "What kind of man are you who loves his offspring more than their mother?"

Forgetting for a second that the child in question was not hers, she demanded, "Who bore you that child? Without your wives would you have any sons at all? How can you think of casting off the very people to whom you owe your sons' existence?"

"You speak as though Rama was your son. You feel offended that I prefer him to his mother, as if you were his mother."

"No! No!" she said vehemently. "He is not my son but Kausalya's son. Bharata is my son, and I want him to rule the world." Every word she said stabbed through his aging heart.

"Nothing makes sense anymore," he said, feeling suddenly tired. "You consider Rama and Bharata on an equal level. I know that because you have told me so many times. Who has turned your mind against Rama? Against me?"

"What is the use of this talk, O King? Are you going to do as you promised or not?"

The king, who ruled the entire earth with an iron hand,

stooped in front of his wife. Thousands of valorous men had kissed his feet during his life, and now he touched the feet of his wife, weeping piteously, begging.

"Have pity on an old man. If not for your husband, who has loved you, have mercy on a man at the end of his life. When I see Rama, supreme delight enters my heart. My very consciousness is lost if I don't see Rama. The world can exist without the sun, crops without water, but life cannot continue in my body without Rama. I beg you to let me die with my son at my side. Let me die in peace."

"How can you die in peace when you have not kept your word of honor?"

Dasharatha clutched at his chest and cried louder. "I will give you the entire earth," he said. "I agree to make Bharata king. He is also my son, although not the eldest. I am ready to hand over this earth to Bharata. I will give you that gladly. But I will not banish Rama. He is faultless and has never hurt either of us nor anyone else. When Rama treats you as he does his own mother, why are you bent on harming him? What kind of wicked heart do you possess, wishing harm on one so pure, who is kind to every being? Has he ever said a single word that displeased you?"

"We are not here to discuss the qualities or lack of qualities of your darling son, King. Stop temporizing and agree, as you must, to both of my wishes."

"Do you really think Bharata will accept this kingdom,

knowing it is rightfully Rama's? He is devoted to Rama... but he is, after all, your son. Maybe his greed will be like yours. And God, how could I have been so blind to your defects? Have I been so blinded by your beauty that I could not see what lurked inside you? Where has all this jealousy and hate come from? You are jealous of an innocent child who loves you. You have changed from my beloved wife to a fanged serpent."

The king's heart wrenched painfully as years of love transformed into something foul and nameless. The pain wracked his entire body, and he felt himself already beginning to die. He saw a slight smile on the woman's lips. Could she see that she had won her battle?

"But at what cost?" he shouted, "At what cost do you win? I will die. You gave my life back so many years ago, it's true, but do you now wish me to die a broken man? This world will curse you as I die, and Rama, my poor Rama, will be exiled from a kingdom that is rightfully his. I can see him wandering in a cold jungle, searching for something to eat, starving, my little prince, my boy. How could I let this happen to him? I will never agree to your evil plan. Never! Cruel woman of wicked nature, you are bent on exterminating our race. What wrong have I or Rama done to you that we deserve this fate at your hands?"

He fainted again in the doorway and awoke only to find that dreadful witch of a woman by his side, making his pain worse with angry words and ridicule. Kaikeyi's heart was stone, and all she felt was disgust for this old man who had

promised so many sweet things in the solitude of her bed chambers but who did not dare fulfil her desires when she finally asked something of him.

"Was this love?" she asked herself bitterly. She had often heard from maidservants about men's deceptions. They were always promising, promising, but never giving what actually mattered. She had rejected those words as the bitter prattle of the unloved, but now she knew they were true. The king had failed his "favorite" queen. All his love had been a joke, an illusion. The truth was that the king had never loved Kaikeyi or her son. Only Rama mattered to him. Maybe her own love for Rama had grown as an unconscious attempt to shield herself from this truth. Thinking in this way, she could not stop the rush of words that aimed to hurt him every time he awoke, and she succeeded more with her sharp tongue than if she had taken a sword to his aged limbs.

Two hearts, once one, separated that night.

"This is my punishment for loving you too much," the king said bitterly. A sense of great shame pierced him for unkind deeds he had done in the name of love, her love. "In the past I've gone to great lengths to fulfill your every whim. But now, if I agree with your wicked plans of harming Rama, the world will scorn me as a love-sick dog. Venerable people will gather in the streets and reproach me for rejecting a son out of lust for a woman. They will scorn me, their once respected king, but they will also scorn you, Kaikeyi. Can't you see this? The world will hate you for this, as I already hate you."

"You speak of hate, but I speak of truth," Kaikeyi persisted. "You are stubbornly avoiding accepting your duty. You simply want to enjoy your life with Kausalya and your son forever."

On hearing the name of his first queen, a new pain stabbed King Dasharatha's heart, and he wailed. "Oh, how will I face that kind woman after sending her son into the jungle? Kausalya, the mother of my dearest son, always speaks kind words. She deserves kind treatment in return, which I have failed to give, doting on you, serpent of a wife. Kausalya has waited on me like a maidservant, a friend, and a wife. She has been like a sister and a mother. But for your sake, I never treated her kindly. I have cruelly ignored her, not wanting to displease you."

Hearing her co-wife praised only increased Kaikeyi's bitterness and her determination to have her boons. "Well, you are severely displeasing me now by your ridiculous refusal to fulfill my requests."

"If I do as you say, Kausalya, Sumitra, and my other three sons, even Bharata, will feel tortured. Having thrown all of us into hell, you, however, will be happy."

Minute by minute, causing each other pain as expertly as they had once loved each other, the king and queen endured the long night thus until sunrise. A decision had to be made. As if thrashing a horse with a whip, Kaikeyi pressed her demands on Dasharatha again and again. She was impatient for her new world to rise, while he wished for the night never to end so he would not have to see the dreams of his old age shattered forever.

A Prince is Exiled

THE SUN ROSE, but the king did not move. During the night he had made his way out of the sulking chambers but had fainted again inside Kaikeyi's chamber. He seemed unable to escape from her. Kaikeyi was standing close by, unmoving and staring. "He has to get up sometime," she thought.

When the morning musicians, who were the royal alarm clock, entered with melodious upbeat tunes, Dasharatha groaned and shouted, "You are increasing my suffering with your noise! Go away." The music stopped abruptly.

Kaikeyi's eyes widened with disbelief. "Does he think he can sleep forever? Is he hoping the situation will go away if he ignores it?" she wondered. Kaikeyi remained where she had been by his side. Her eyes were livid, and she wanted the king to rise and face his duty. She searched for something to say that would provoke him to action, but she had run out of daggers. She continued to stand by him, silent and waiting, like death's crone.

Outside others were also waiting for the king. The installation was set to begin. Where was the king? Sumantra was sent to inquire. He marched up the palace hallway and continued on to Kaikeyi's quarters. Sumantra stopped in the doorway when he saw Dasharatha lying on the floor. Surprised, he greeted the king ceremoniously and declared that Vasishta had arrived and that the ceremony was ready to begin.

"O King, arise!" he exhorted. "All preparations have been made. The people are eagerly awaiting your arrival."

No answer.

Kaikeyi's eyes glittered dangerously as she spoke. "The king is not feeling well. He wants to see Rama immediately."

"Your Majesty?"

"Immediately, I said," Kaikeyi answered.

Sumantra was not at all obliged to take orders from Kaikeyi, but his sharp eyes had noted the contrast between the queen's animated face and the king's withdrawn and pained expression. Something was wrong. Maybe Rama could sort it out. Sumantra acceded to Rama's judiciousness, despite his youth. He backed out of the doorway to seek him out.

Dasharatha moaned, "No!" to the empty doorway.

The king opened his eyes, which also glittered dangerously.

"You wicked, foul witch, destroyer of our family. You are no longer my wife. I abandon your hand, which was clasped by me in marriage before the sacred fire. Do you hear me? You are not my wife. I forbid you to touch me or to approach me. You have no right to stand here. Get out of my sight."

"Ha, have it your way. If I had been interested in romance, I would have asked you to abandon those two other creatures you call wife." She crossed the room and stood as far away from him as the room allowed. "But that's obviously not what I want, and I will have what I want whether you do your part or not, King. Why are you hesitating to follow the path of righteousness? How will you be able to face the world, having denied me these boons? Do not violate your pledge to me. It is by my grace that you are still alive, and this is how you thank me?"

"Like a woman who has been perverted by an evil spirit, you are not ashamed of speaking to me in this way, making worthless things seem worthwhile. How can you insist on righteousness when what you ask for is abominable?" King Dasharatha got up slowly and laboriously and sat on a cushioned couch facing the door, waiting for Rama to arrive. "Rama must be on his way now. Rama, my darling son, is incapable of disregarding my command. If I ask him to go to the forest, he will do so. Oh, if only he would act contrary to my decree, it would be most welcome. But he will never do that. Oh, why did the sun rise today?"

By that time Sumantra had reached Rama's palace and saw the citizens who were crowding there, waiting for Rama to emerge for his installation. The previous night had not been an idle one for the citizens, who had been decorating the city. Flower garlands were wrapped around every pillar, and colourful flags fluttered in the breeze. They were burning aloe wood to enhance the auspicious atmosphere. Sumantra noted that they were dressed beautifully, equalling the sun in splendour. Uniformed soldiers lined the steps of the entrance to Rama's palace. No one stopped or questioned Sumantra because he was so well respected by the king. Sumantra entered the inner chamber and saw Rama and Sita dressed in fine silks seated together on a throne. His right hand played with a lotus-flower, the other rested on Sita's knee. Though Sumantra saw Rama often, he was taken aback by the loveliness of their combination.

Rama was as strong and solid as Sita was soft and delicate.

Like the pinkish lotus in his hand, Sita's feminity emphasized Rama's broad shoulders and upper arms. The slenderness of his youth had given way to a physique that accurately reflected his mental maturation and strength. The definition of his muscles and the calluses on his hands spoke of his dedication to his Kshatriya duties.

The couple both stood up respectfully when they saw Sumantra approach. The minister conveyed the king's summon. Rama turned to Sita.

"Father and Kaikeyi must want to bless me personally before the ceremony begins. Wait for me here, I will come back for you soon."

When the two men emerged from the palace, the people cheered. Lakshmana was standing at the outer gate with folded hands. Rama greeted him fondly and told him of the king's summons.

A chariot drawn by four horses stood waiting to take Rama to his installation; waving to the people who surrounded it, Rama mounted the chariot. Lakshmana jumped on behind as they sped off toward the king's palace. Driving through the clean streets, Rama saw how expectant the people were. Whoever saw him shouted words of praise or shed tears of joy, and the lion-hearted roared their approval. Beautiful women sprinkled flowers from their balconies as he passed. Their love for him was as enormous as the ocean.

Rama, glowing like a second sun, entered Kaikeyi's chambers followed by Sumantra; Lakshmana remained outside, since he had not been summoned. Seeing his father sitting on the couch and Kaikeyi standing next to him, Rama smiled broadly and went forward. The king was still, and his eyes were shut; however, it was evident that he was not asleep.

"You called for me, father?" Rama asked. He bowed low, touching the king's feet first, and then Kaikeyi's. This was the greeting of respect Rama and his brothers had all used the moment they were old enough to realize that their father was not only their father but the king.

Rama's forehead was painted with the emblems of the Sun dynasty—a half-sun with its golden rays reaching up toward his hairline. His hair was still wet from his morning ablutions, and it curled attractively around his ears. He had not expected to go anywhere but to the sacrificial arena for the installation, and his fine dress and attractive appearance reflected this.

Dasharatha opened his eyes and looked straight at his son, then immediately averted his eyes as they brimmed with tears. Looking like an eclipsed sun, the king had lost his luster. He continued to avoid Rama's face as tears streamed down his cheeks. Rama became alarmed. He had never seen his father like this. Since the king was silent and consciously avoiding his eyes, Rama voiced his concern to Kaikeyi.

"Father's face is full of anguish, as if he has committed an abominable act. What has caused this? In the past, he has always brightened to see me, but today he looks ill. Have I done something to displease him? If so, I do not wish to live for a moment without satisfying him or fulfilling his desire. Please tell me what is wrong."

Kaikeyi smiled as she saw the fulfillment of her goal approach. At least Rama would adhere to her wishes. She knew it but didn't stop to think why she so much wanted to harm the one whose loyalty and devotion she relied on. The king was evidently not going to speak. "I will do it myself," she thought.

"Rama, your father is not ill. He is like this because he wants something from you but is afraid to tell you for fear of hurting you."

"Afraid?" Rama smiled in surprise. "How could that be? I have never seen my father afraid of anything. And have I ever neglected to follow his orders in any way?"

Kaikeyi's heart soared at his words. She pounced on the opportunity to explain in detail the history of her two boons. She was cleverly appealing to Rama's well-known and strong sense of righteousness. Once a promise was made, it could never be broken. She related the history of her two boons and then came to her conclusion.

"I have asked your father to fulfill these two boons, but because of his unmanly weakness, he has taken refuge in silence. Rama, you must heed your father's words. I will tell you my desires if you promise to carry them out."

" I am prepared to die for my father. Please speak freely about what he has promised because I shall carry out whatever he wishes. This is my solemn promise."

"My son, Bharata, will take your place as king, and you will be exiled to the forest for fourteen years, wearing only deerskin and living like a recluse. These are my two wishes."

The expression on Kaikeyi's face was cruel, but there was no change in Rama's demeanor.

Sumantra's expression, however, revealed his shock; he had not imagined the depth of the king's despair or his predicament. His heart hammered against his chest. Until now he had held Kaikeyi in the highest esteem, but this injustice went against all good sense. The people of Ayodhya would be devastated. Sumantra looked at Rama, who was looking at the silent figure of his father. Rama did not yet comprehend his mother's sudden enmity or his father's silence, but the king's agony was clear. Rama did not want to aggravate the situation. If it were true that the king wished

Bharata to rule, but was simply afraid to say it openly, Rama did not want to hurt his father by displaying any emotion. He kept his face impassive. Yet his eyes were alert to any clue revealing his father's actual desire.

"So, will you do your duty?" Kaikeyi pressed, "even though the king is bent on following an unrighteous path by refusing to grant my wishes?"

"I will fulfill all my father's promises to you. Send messengers for Bharata so that he may take my place at the installation. I will proceed to the forest."

A painful moan escaped the king's lips as Rama acceded to Kaikeyi's demands.

Suddenly animated, Kaikeyi exclaimed, "Yes! Let messengers on the swiftest horses be sent at once to bring my son home. And you, Rama, I don't think it's good for you to delay the beginning of your exile. Go to the forest at once."

"Mother, be delighted for I will, without a doubt, do as you say. However, do not become indignant if I tarry for a moment by my father's side. Indeed, happily will I do as you command, but my heart is aching because my father has not personally told me of his wishes. Why is he gazing steadily at the floor? Why are tears flowing from his eyes?"

"Do not concern yourself with your father. He is too mortified to open his mouth, since you are his pet son. I advise you to leave as soon as possible. Until you leave, he will not recover himself. I doubt he'll be able to eat breakfast or bathe until you are out of the city."

King Dasharatha fainted when he heard Kaikeyi's words. He would not continue to live. Seeing his father in a faint, Rama ran forward and lifted him. His brow furrowed as he set his father upright on the couch again. He understood clearly now that the proceedings were contrary to his father's true wishes. Rama had grown to manhood without ever seeing his father so vulnerable. He kept his arms around his father even after the king was secure in his seat. His handsome face bore signs of concern, and for the first time he reproved Kaikeyi mildly.

"I am not a slave of passion or greed, Mother. I would gladly have given you the kingdom had you only asked. What was the need to trouble my father? You know that I will always obey you. You could have simply asked me."

Kaikeyi did not acknowledge his words but simply emphasized again that he hasten to leave. Implored by Kaikeyi, Rama reluctantly let go of his feeble father and left the room.

A Mother's Sorrow

EMERGING FROM KAIKEYI'S chamber, Rama saw Lakshmana pacing furiously. Lakshmana's knuckles were white from clenching his fists, and his eyes were an explosion of red. Lakshmana was much quicker to anger than Rama and was, in many other ways, his opposite. Rama was a perfect gentleman under all circumstances, but Lakshmana complemented Rama's calm nature with his own impassioned one. He was ready to burst with fury for the injustice done to his brother. However, Rama did not give him the chance to explode as he hurried to Kausalya's palace. Lakshmana had no choice but to follow Rama's rushed steps; he didn't dare interrupt his brother's silence.

Rama, who was greatly hurt, sighed deeply as he proceeded to his mother's chambers. He wanted to inform her personally about his exile because he feared for her life if she heard the news from anyone else. Before entering

Kausalya's chambers, Rama schooled his face to calmness. He must be prepared to see the shock and pain of those close to him without compounding it with his own. In truth, he had only accepted the throne out of duty. He was not disturbed that this duty was transferred to another. The pain he felt came from Kaikeyi's transformation and his father's anguish. The order must be carried out, but it was obvious that it was not what the king wanted. Rama realized that by carrying out the order, he was actually hurting his father, but there was no other choice.

Kaikeyi's deception lay heavy on his heart because he had always loved her as his mother. Rama knew she must have manipulated the king. Despite this, he remembered how often Kaikeyi had loved him and showered him with her affection. This one instance could not erase those memories. Rama did not want Kausalya to know of his anguish, so he curtained off his mind as he walked into her quarters.

He saw his mother, who had grown lean due to her observance of vows, dressed in a cream and gold sari. She looked pure and happy even before her face brightened upon his arrival. Before she could praise him or express happiness about this day, however, he quickly told her what had just occurred. Kausalya dropped to the floor, her sari fluttering around her as she fell, her face losing its luster.

She cried out, "I would not have felt this grief had I been childless! Rama, since you were a child I have nourished you. I have spent sleepless nights caring for you and anxious days guiding your steps. I have busied my days with prayers for you and have observed vows for your success. And it comes to this? This is not fair, my son. You cannot be exiled! What is your crime? You have never hurt anyone."

Kausalya's face became distorted as emotions she had never meant to reveal surfaced. "Oh, that malicious Kaikeyi! This is all her doing! It hasn't been enough to taunt me through the years, flaunting herself before me as she gathered the king's love to her bosom. She wants to utterly destroy me by sending you far away from me. Wouldn't it be enough to put her own son on the throne? But why, Rama, is she exiling you to the forest? Although I knew she was spiteful and arrogant, I didn't doubt her love for you. Has she only pretended that love for all these years? Oh, Rama, don't go. I have been rejected by the king and insulted by my co-wives again and again, but I had you, so I tolerated everything. You don't know how Kaikeyi will torture me when you are gone! Because of you, I have survived, and without you, I cannot live. I will come with you."

"Mother, please," Rama stroked her back. "You know Bharata. He will not let any harm befall you. I am sure of this. He is virtuous and kind. And think about Father. He is old now. Kaikeyi has deceived him, and if you too abandon him, how will he survive? The duty of a wife is to remain beside her husband. You must stay."

"Then you too must stay. I will not allow you to go!" Kausalya cried in his arms like a child who would not be soothed. Rama was deeply grieved to see his mother's condition.

"Please do not cry. I cannot bear to see you like this. Please give me your blessings so that I may go and return safely. I promise that I will come back to you after the fourteen years are over."

Lakshmana could not control himself any longer. "Mother, I also cannot accept Rama listening to the words of that vulgar woman. I want you to know that I am loyal to Rama and Rama alone. It seems that the old king has become a plaything in Kaikeyi's hands. The king has become senile, controlled by lust and old age, and he will now do anything Kaikeyi proposes. I will not stand by while my brother is robbed of what is rightfully his. I am ready to take up my sword and fight for the throne. If anyone tries to stop me I will annihilate the entire city! I swear, if the king is against us, I am ready to kill even him!"

"Lakshmana," Rama said, alarmed, "I know your loyalty to me is unbreakable, and I don't doubt your strength. But don't be angry with father. A father should always be respected and loved no matter what he does."

"No, Rama, a guru or even a father who has gone astray should be rejected. I say Father has proven, beyond all doubt, that he is not capable of following righteousness any longer. He should be rejected accordingly."

"Lakshmana, you are angry. But has Father ever been unjust before this day? Have you ever seen him follow evil ways? No, he has taught us everything we know about goodness, and we should never forget this. He is not doing this out of some misplaced attachment to Kaikeyi. I swear my life on it. You didn't see him, Lakshmana. He is suffering more than we are. He has been trapped."

"I cannot understand you, Rama. You are forgetting your Kshatriya spirit. You should fight for what is yours. Instead you have become a mouse. You must fight this injustice and kill your enemies."

Speaking as much to his inconsolable mother as to his brother, Rama said, "Brother, we are not speaking of enemies but of our father and mother. Hold back your grief and anger, Lakshmana. Forget these insults and gather courage instead. Revenge is never a commendable path. Even if our father has wronged us, we must not wrong him in return. Better to act without fault. I do not remember ever having displeased any of my elders, and I will not begin today. Don't blame Kaikeyi for this. Kaikeyi's drastic change in behavior toward us and her husband must have been caused by fate. I see no other explanation for her sudden animosity, for neither have I ever harmed her nor has she been unhappy with me before today."

"Kaikeyi! That snake!"

"Lakshmana, has she not been a mother to us? I love my mothers equally because each one loved me fully and raised me carefully. We should always respect them for this no matter what they do later on. Kaikeyi is a tool of fate and in no way less esteemed by me despite her apparent treachery. Don't work against me, Lakshmana."

"You talk of fate, but enthroning someone other than you will not please the people. I cannot tolerate it, Rama."

"The people will become satisfied as soon as Bharata is on the throne and they see that he is a good king. I must be far away from here before peace can return. The people will not accept Bharata while I am still here. That's why I insist, Mother, that you give me your blessings now. Messengers have already been sent to bring Bharata home. I must leave as soon as possible."

Seeing how both his mother and brother opposed him, Rama became stern. "Lakshmana, now you are joining sides with Mother against me without considering my opinion. Let our father's promise become true. I will go to the forest wearing deerskin and matted hair for his sake. I go to honor our father's promise."

Turning next to his mother, Rama pleaded, "Mother, please do not make this hard for me. I am determined to protect my father's honor. But I cannot go without your blessings. Please grant them to me."

Kausalya had watched Rama soothe Lakshmana and had listened to his words. Quivering with unshed tears, she gave him her blessings, calling out to all the elements of the cosmos to protect him. "May the path of righteousness that you are walking protect you, my son. May the knowledge of weapons you gained from Vishvamitra protect you. May the sun and moon, as well as the day and night, protect you. May the rivers you cross, the trees under which you walk, the flowers on your path, and the animals protect you. May all the world protect you, and may you return safely. My blessings are with you."

Kausalya then embraced Rama and, pulling his head down, smelled and kissed the top of his head. Rama touched her feet again and again. With a heavy heart he proceeded home, accompanied by Lakshmana, to take leave of his beloved Sita.

Taking Farewell of His Princess

WHEN RAMA ENTERED his inner chambers, he saw Sita exactly where he had left her hours ago, waiting faithfully for him. Her face was tranquil, so Rama knew that she did not yet know what had happened. He would have to explain everything to her, but how? When he felt such pain, how would he spare her? Anticipating her despair, he felt his resolve weaken for a moment. He could pretend to be immune in front of other people but not in front of Sita who had spent the past ten years learning his every gesture. Seeing her, he could not contain his emotions.

Sita was startled by the paleness of his face. She quickly ran up to him and became even more concerned when she saw that he was perspiring. "Rama, my love, what has happened? Something dreadful must have befallen you."

Rama stood silently, his hands hanging by his sides.

"I see that you have come alone," she reasoned. "None of the appointed people are accompanying you as they should on this day. You have come back adorned as you left. Why has no one garlanded you or put sacred marks on your forehead? Something is wrong, I know, yet you stand silently. This frightens me more than anything else." She bit her lip and looked down. "Rama, why are you clenching your jaw? Is it because you wish to spare me unpleasant news? Rama, don't keep anything from me, for I am as ready to share your sorrow as I am to share your happiness. Don't hesitate to share your burden with me."

Rama suddenly embraced Sita and took comfort from her for a few seconds before composing himself. Then he began the painful task of saying goodbye. "Sita, Kaikeyi commands that Bharata take my place on the throne and I be exiled to the forest for fourteen years. I must leave at once. I have simply come to see you one last time before departing. Listen, sweetest Sita. You must listen to whatever Bharata orders so that you do not incur his wrath. Do not praise me in front of him. And don't neglect your elders when I am gone. Pay your respects to my father every day, and in this way immerse your mind in pious acts. The fourteen years will pass quickly."

Sita's eyes blazed with anger. She did not care about the throne, but how could he speak of separating from her? "I should laugh at what you have just said, dear husband. How can you talk of going anywhere without me? Wherever you go, I shall follow."

Rama took her by the shoulders and held her at arm's length. Looking squarely into her eyes, he tried to explain himself. "Sita, my lovely wife, the forest is no place for a woman, especially not a princess. The ground is hard, and your soft body will be bruised by it. You will not be able to sleep at all because of the scorpions and snakes that crawl over those who sleep on the ground. The torrential rains will soak you and ruin the silkiness of your skin and hair. You will have only roots, leaves, and the seasonal fruits to eat. Just hearing the growls of tigers will frighten you. Crocodiles will snap at your ankles as we cross streams and rivers. These are just a few of the austerities you'll have to endure. You will constantly be subjected to the dangers of the unpredictable jungle. How will you tolerate it?"

"I do not care about dangers as long as I am by your side. Staying here without you will be hell. I do not care what troubles I must undergo as long as I can be with you."

"If I took you along, I would be endangering your life. I cannot accept that, my beloved. The jungle is full of man-eating animals seeking prey. You are the sweetest of graceful women. Seeing you, the ferocious animals will be attracted and mistake you for a most enchanting deer. They will surely attack you. The jungle is no place for a lovely woman like you, Sita."

"Dear Rama, if they will be attracted to me, they will flee on seeing you. If I am by your side, would you really have me believe I am in danger?"

"Sita, I cannot take you with me. If anything happened to you..."

"How can you be sure I am safe here?" Sita was truly angry

now. “A woman alone without her husband! You abandon me and talk about my safety? Oh,” she sobbed into her hands, “why did my father choose you for his son-in-law? A wife’s place is by her husband’s side. Have I ever displeased you that you would think of abandoning me now? The people of Ayodhya are wrong to praise you as the incarnation of virtue. You are cruel and hard-hearted. How can you leave me here and go away for fourteen years? Without you, Rama, without you I cannot live.”

Sita took Rama’s hand and pressed it to her heart urgently. “Dear husband, I will walk in front of you and trample the thorns on the path so they don’t hurt your feet. I will pick fruits for you from the trees. I will not displease you in any way, I promise. I will enjoy seeing the waterfalls and hearing the sounds of exotic animals.”

“But Sita, those same waterfalls will frighten you when darkness falls and you hear them rumbling through the night. Animals will growl, and other mysterious noises will make you anxious.”

Sita clutched Rama’s shoulders and looked up into his face, “Please…” she whispered, “don’t leave me.”

Rama’s jaw clenched again, but he took a step away, shrugging her hands off. “Sita, you know I have to go. Don’t make this so hard.”

“You are the one making it hard by leaving me here!” Sita cried. She was beginning to feel dizzy with fear as she thought of being separated from Rama. If someone had thrown her into a black hole with no hope of ever emerging, she could not have felt more forlorn. Her sobs shook her body, and tears burst from her large eyes.

"If you leave me here, I will end my life by drinking poison. You will come back to find me dead. Be sure of this."

"Sita!" He grabbed her close and saved her from falling.

She sobbed into his chest. "I cannot live without you. I cannot. And I would rather end my life than live here without you."

He quieted her then and hugged her tightly, feeling he would never let her go. For her safety and comfort he had wanted her to stay in Ayodhya, but he knew she would be happier by his side. He could find no more reasons to leave her behind. "Sita, don't cry. I will take you along. How would I be at peace in the forest knowing you were alone and unhappy?"

She smiled weakly, looking up at him through her tears. Those few words immediately soothed her.

"I had to try to dissuade you because life in the forest will be austere. You have to know what we will face as we leave Ayodhya behind. I had to see the state of your mind. Sita, life in the forest will not be easy."

She simply smiled at him now and wiped away her tears.

"Go at once and distribute all your belongings. Prepare for our departure. I will do the same. Then we will go and bid my father farewell."

Sita set out swiftly to give away all that she possessed.

They would start their life as forest-dwellers with no material belongings. Rama had no sooner stepped out of the door than he found Lakshmana at his feet, pleading, "Take me with you."

As he had done with Sita, Rama presented the difficulties that they would face in the jungle and tried to dissuade Lakshmana from coming. However, Lakshmana would by no means be discouraged from following Rama. "No, Rama, I will walk in front of you and Sita and make sure no wild animals are around. In this way, you both can enjoy the scenery undisturbed. I will pick fruits from the trees for you when you are hungry, and I will guard you both when you sleep."

Rama was not surprised to hear Lakshmana's plea, and he finally relented. He had been prepared to bear his exile alone, but after seeing their strong resolve to accompany him, he had to admit he felt content. The exile would not be a torture when the two he most loved would be with him.

"Then go, Lakshmana, and bid farewell to your mother and wife. Give away your belongings as Sita and I are doing. We will then go to Father's palace and bid him farewell."

The Final Farewell

OUTSIDE, IN THE streets of Ayodhya, the people were crowding together. The news of Kaikeyi's deception and Rama's exile had circulated. The few people who had been inside their houses when the installation was due to take place were called out by their neighbors. Everyone was incredulous. A few old men stood together shaking their heads in disbelief, but the groups of younger men were more agitated. Shaking their fists in the air or pounding each other on the back, they seemed uncertain how to react. The women openly sobbed and consoled one another. The same beautiful women who had showered flowers on Rama from their balconies now lay prostrate on those same balconies like wilted flowers. Ayodhya had never witnessed such a tragedy. Rama was not going to be king.

Sita, Rama, and Lakshmana were greeted with the sight of people hugging and lamenting as they set out on foot to Dasharatha's palace. The cries became louder when the people saw the king of their hearts walking like a common man, his wife following him. Until then Sita had not been seen in the public eye. A princess of her stature always travelled in a covered palanquin. It was not with happiness that the people saw her now. Many of the elders covered their eyes. Under different circumstances the people would certainly have been struck by her loveliness; now they thought only of her departure with Rama.

A cry arose from the crowd. "Don't go! Don't go!"

The shout was heard from every corner, and Lakshmana could not help but clench his fists with suppressed anger and look at his elder brother imploringly. Rama gazed ahead steadily but smiled now and then to the people as he passed. As they walked, the citizens began to follow, and by the time they reached King Dasharatha's palace, thousands of distressed citizens were gathered behind them.

When the threesome entered the palace, King Dasharatha rose to embrace Rama. Many, including the queens and ministers, had gathered in the room to witness Rama's farewell or, if possible, to prevent it. The king was delirious with grief, his once-erect back now bent with the burden of self-reproach. He did not have the energy to carry himself across the room to greet Rama, collapsing halfway.

The servants in attendance sobbed, and Sita closed her eyes when she saw her father-in-law's condition. Sumantra had to leave the room for some minutes to compose himself. Rama and Lakshmana ran up to their father. Each took an arm and lifted him. Then Lakshmana's lips began to tremble. After seating their father, Lakshmana grabbed a fan from one of the servants and fanned his father while swallowing his tears.

When King Dasharatha regained his composure, he looked at Rama and implored, "Rama, imprison me at once! Take the throne by force! No one will stop you!"

"Father, please. Do not feel that you have hurt me. I shall go to the forest happily, knowing that I am fulfilling your promise. I don't care about the throne. Satisfying your promise is the only thing dear to me."

Deep down in his honorable heart, King Dasharatha knew that his promise to Kaikeyi could not and should not be broken. Rama was insisting on fulfilling the vow, despite the king's loud remonstrance to the contrary. Rama knew that a promise should never be broken. The king had at one time said that something would be so, and so it must be.

When the king saw that Rama was determined to go, he wanted to make sure he went comfortably. "Sumantra, make arrangements for a portion of my army to accompany Rama. Select some of the best servants, merchants, and cooks. Let them arrange for large tents and many cushions and soft blankets. If my son must go to the forest, let him go in royal comfort."

"You can't do this!" Kaikeyi exclaimed. She had been silent until this moment. There had been no need for her to interfere, since everything was running smoothly according to her desires. When she heard the king's order, her mouth dried up and she became afraid. "He is trying to trick me," she thought.

"You are trying to take what belongs to my son. Bharata will never accept a land robbed of its plenty!"

"Be quiet, woman! Why do you want to poke a hot iron into the wounds you have already created? If you didn't want me to send Rama in comfort, you should have included that in your boons."

Kaikeyi's eyes grew cold, and she said callously, "King, there is a precedent in our dynasty for how a son should be exiled. King Sagara cast off his son, Asamanja, without anything. You should do the same to Rama."

The room became heavy with silence. How had Kaikeyi become so cold-hearted?

One of the senior ministers, a man with a long white beard, began to shake with indignation. "Kaikeyi, Asamanja took delight in drowning his playmates in the Sarayu River. When the citizens complained, King Sagara cast him off. How dare you compare Asamanja to Rama, who has never spoken an ill word or harmed anyone. King Sagara acted in accordance with his people's wishes. Can you claim that you are doing the same? You should end this evil charade before it goes too far."

Kaikeyi stared at the old minister with undiminished disdain. Almost all the elders had already personally pleaded with her to change her will. They could see no other way out of this calamity. Although Kaikeyi was unmoved by the minister's words, King Dasharatha was not.

"Yes, if you go on with your plan Kaikeyi, I will take all my people with me and will myself accompany Rama to the forest. You can stay here and enjoy the kingdom with your son. The citizens will never follow you when their hearts are with Rama."

Before Kaikeyi could protest, Rama broke in. "No, Father, I shall go to the forest alone as Kaikeyi has decreed. Sita and Lakshmana are determined to follow me, although I have tried to dissuade them. Please give us your permission to go at once. I am sure peace will be restored as soon as Kaikeyi's boons are carried out, as they must be, Father."

When King Dasharatha heard the finality in Rama's words, his life-air lost its purpose, and he fainted once again. Kaikeyi, however, wasted no time on the king, for she wanted Rama out of her kingdom before he changed his mind. She went immediately to bring the deerskin and tree-bark cloth she had acquired and presented them to Rama, Sita, and Lakshmana. They should go like true ascetics.

When Sita tried to put on the rough cloth and was confused about how to wrap it around her body, everyone in the room began to cry. It was heart wrenching to see the beautiful princess accept the humble clothing so willingly, she who was born for a life of comfort and whose skin was accustomed to the finest silks. Many audibly cursed Kaikeyi.

Sumantra was then ordered to fetch the chariot. Rama, Sita, and Lakshmana touched their elders' feet. Dasharatha was ashamed to face his daughter-in-law, but when Sita reached out and took his hand, he clasped both her hands to his chest and said, "Forgive me," again and again. Sita's serene face and compassionate tears soothed him for some moments.

Lakshmana, who had remained in the background, threw himself at his father's feet. Dasharatha stroked Lakshmana's head, and they embraced. Meanwhile, Rama singled out his own mother and brought her forward to his father.

"Father, I have one request to make of you before I leave. Here is my mother, your faithful wife. Watch over her carefully and do not allow any harm to befall her from anyone, especially from her co-wives. She is now bereft of her only son, and I beg you to take care of her."

Kausalya's face was drenched in tears, and King Dasharatha nodded and hung his head in shame. Rama then went forward to embrace his father one last time, and the king took him in his arms and refused to let go.

Kausalya turned to Sita. "Sita, it is well known that women forget about past happy years as soon as misfortune sets in. They may even leave righteous husbands in favor of a more opulent position. Please do not abandon my son in his misfortune. Now that he is in exile, do not become bitter toward him. Keep him always close to your heart."

"Please do not talk about unfaithful women to me, Mother," Sita replied fiercely, "for my happiness is only in Rama, and I don't even want to hear advice about remaining faithful to him. It hurts me to even think of a life without Rama. Please do not worry, for I will do my best to keep him happy in the forest."

The two women hugged, and Sita held Kausalya's hand firmly to reassure her. King Dasharatha's arms were still tightly wrapped around his beloved son. Pain etched deep lines on his face. Rama finally disengaged himself from his father's arms and took Sita's hand. Taking Lakshmana's hand as well, Rama led them out to the waiting chariot.

"Please start at once," Rama requested Sumantra, who had decided to personally serve as their charioteer. Rama didn't want to see his sobbing mother and father standing on the street as he left, but he did see the citizens mourning his departure, pathetically hanging onto the chariot trying to detain their prince. The chariot's start was a slow one. It gradually picked up speed as Rama tried to soothe the people around him.

"Stop the chariot!"

Sumantra's head whipped around when he heard the shout. Rama turned around and saw his father running through the crowd crying, "Stop the chariot! Stop the chariot!" Sumantra habitually heeded his master's command.

"What are you doing?" Rama cried over his shoulder. "Speed up!"

Confused by the contradictory instructions, Sumantra didn't know what to do. He had lived his life following the king's orders. He slowed the chariot. The king, who was weak and exhausted, ran pitifully behind. It was a heartbreaking sight. Rama's composure broke and he shouted.

"Can't you see that it is unbearable for me to see my aged father like this? Speed up the chariot and end this at once!"

Sumantra cracked his whip and urged the horses on. Sita took Rama's shoulder and firmly turned him back until he was facing the direction they were going, saving him from seeing King Dasharatha stumble in the dust and fall. The chariot sped forever out of Dasharatha's reach.

Kausalya and Kaikeyi ran forward to help him.

"You! Don't touch me! You are not my wife! I already told you. And I say for all to hear, if Bharata goes along with your scheme, he is no longer my son. I do not want him near me in life, and he may not perform my funeral rites. Get out of my sight!"

Kaikeyi was stung and visibly paled. She stepped aside, and the king said, "Take me to Kausalya's chambers. I will remain there from now on."

A few people glared at Kaikeyi with hatred, but most people looked at the dust caused by Rama's disappearing chariot. The prince who was to be their king was gone.

Confessions of a Dying King

INTERMINABLE HOURS HAD passed since Rama's chariot had disappeared over the horizon. The king, who had been repeatedly calling out for his son, was taken to Kausalya's bedchambers as he had requested. He was growing weaker as his life drained out of him. He spoke only of his firstborn son.

"Rama is quite an archer, you know," he said, but instead of elaborating on Rama's qualities, he surprised Kausalya and Sumitra by turning the subject to himself. "I was not half bad either when I was his age. It's amusing to reflect on how much we value things that are so transitory," he said. "I took great pride in my archery in those days. Now I would miss an elephant standing in front of me."

"That's not true," Kausalya burst out loyally, but instantly closed her mouth when she saw his hand groping in the air toward her. His eyes were staring, but unseeing. Clasping his fumbling hand to her cheek, she kissed his knuckles and tasted salt where the tears from her cheek had rubbed off. How quickly he had become so old. Sumitra, too, was shaken on seeing the king's condition. Her face was averted, but Kausalya could see her shoulders tremble and felt her own sorrow increase as she tried to be strong for all three of them.

"Don't humor me now, dear wife. I know my life is ending. I can feel every step that Rama is taking away from me, and the further he goes, the less I can bear to live. My Rama, so devoid of pride...not like his father," he added, surprising them again by drawing the subject back to himself.

"I knew this day would come. I'm not talking about my death," he chuckled. "Only fools think they will never die. No, I knew I would die a broken man without my son by my side." Kausalya and Sumitra exchanged glances. What was he talking about? Was he losing his mind with grief?

"Kausalya, Sumitra, take my hands. Touch me. I feel so cold." They did as he asked, inching closer and massaging his hands. "I committed a great crime once. It chills my soul to remember it, and so I have never spoken of it. But I must tell you what it was so you can understand."

The two women continued to rub his hands, waiting in silence for his confession. "Oh, how young I was, and how proud of my skill with a bow. Maybe if I hadn't been so rash in my pride—if I hadn't taken such delight in my tricks! The incident happened long before I was married. Hunting was my favorite pastime. I used to spend many hours alone in the forest, shooting faraway targets and practicing my aim. It had become dark that day, just like it is now."

Sumitra bit her lip as the sun's last rays illuminated her tear-streaked face.

"I heard a gurgling sound ahead of me where I knew a stream to be. I took it for the noise of an animal drinking water. What an opportunity to practice my skill at hitting an invisible target. Without a moment's hesitation I grabbed my bow and aimed at the sound. Oh!" A deep groan escaped his cracked lips. "I was gripped by horror to hear a cry of agony echo through the dark night. I ran toward the sound as fast as I could, hoping I was mistaken."

He paused, recalling what he had found at the stream. "It was a boy," he finally said. Kausalya dropped his hand. "Oh, I hit my mark all right," he went on bitterly:

My arrow had gone straight to his heart. By the time I reached him he was already dying. His eyes were rolling back in their sockets, but he struggled to speak to me.

"My parents," he said, "cannot survive without me. Promise me that you will tell them what happened. What if they think I have abandoned them?"

Even though he was in such pain and knew he was dying, this young boy, hardly fifteen, thought only of his parents. I promised him I would inform them, and he begged me to remove the arrow that was causing him such pain. I knew if I pulled it out he would die, but I did it anyway, to end his suffering. I didn't even know his name. Then I saw the water pot floating on the water. He had been filling it at the stream, creating the noise I had heard. I cursed myself and my fate as I filled his pot with water. As I heard that noise again, I cursed my ears. How could I mistake this sound for an animal's thirst? I had no choice but to leave his body at the stream and to search for his parents. I soon found them—two enfeebled elders sitting in a dimly lit hut.

I was afraid to enter the hut and face them, yet I could not bear to stand in the darkness with the filled water pot and to hear them talk about him, the boy I killed. The murder of the young boy lay heavy on me. Now that I am a father, bereaved of my own son, my offense feels unbearable.

"Why is he delaying?" his mother asked.

"Oh, he will come, don't worry," his father replied. "How good he is, our son, taking care of two useless creatures like us, blind and immobile as we are."

"Yes, without him we would surely die within days for lack of water or food."

Then they talked lovingly of times when the roles had been reversed—when he had depended on them for survival. Every word is imprinted in my memory. It was obvious that they lived only for the love of their son.

Kausalya, I was shaking with remorse. Then when I heard his mother once again ask in worried tones when he would come back, I could stand silent no longer. I went inside, ready to throw myself at their feet and beg for forgiveness. But their expectant faces stunned me once again as they heard my arrival.

"Son, is that you?" the old father asked me. "What took you so long? Your mother was worried."

"Oh, but he's back now," she said happily. "Come bring the water to your old mother's lips. I'm so thirsty."

I went forward and put the pot to her lips. She drank a little but immediately asked, "Why are you silent? Your behavior is so unusual. Are you angry with us? Have you tired of caring for your old parents?"

They waited with patient expressions on their faces for me to answer them with loving words. What a son he must have been! Finally I found the courage to do what I had first wanted to do. I threw myself at their feet and cried, "Forgive this wretched sinner!"

"Who are you? Where is our son?" they asked, drawing together and away from me.

Delaying no further, I said, "I am the killer of your son." I quickly told them of my mistake and about the promise I had made to their son before he died. They asked me to bring them to his body. I led them there and then stood silently, watching them cry like small children. Still, they hardly spoke to me. Their silence was painful.

"We are helpless without our son," the father at last said. "Better we die now than wait for slow starvation."

They rejected my offer to personally care for them. The boy's mother said, "We cannot bear to live without our son." I could see that they had lost all desire to live. Deprived of their child, I could see them withering before my eyes.

They asked me to build the boy a funeral pyre and told me that they would give up their lives in the fire. I was powerless to stop them. Before they entered the blazing fire they pronounced a curse on me.

"You have deprived two old parents of their only comfort. Like us, you too will suffer death without your son to comfort you. May you die a bitter death, alone." Those were their last words, and they are coming true.

Kausalya wanted to tell her husband that he wasn't going to die, that he would regain his vitality, but she couldn't deceive herself or the king. Indeed, just as the king saw the boy's parents withering before his eyes, the two queens were witnessing the same happen to Dasharatha. His face was pale and lifeless, and his vision was already going.

"It's getting darker," he said, chilling their hearts.

Kausalya held his hand tightly; she was not yet prepared to let him go. She felt she had just now gained him back and was glad that at least the king had not repented his harsh words to Kaikeyi and remembered his old love in his dying moments. She did not want to share her husband with that witch.

Despite the dying king's confession, Kausalya blamed Kaikeyi for all that had happened in the last twenty-four hours. How easily Kaikeyi had shattered endless years of peace, along with the dream of more to come.

"Rama, Rama," she heard Dasharatha murmur.

How could she soothe him when her own mind echoed his. Where was Rama now? Were his feet being bruised on the jungle paths? Had he found anything to eat? How could he bear to sleep on the hard ground?

As if reading her mind, Dasharatha said, "Rama, your feet must be walking over rocks and thorns. Crush your feet down on my chest. My heart must be like a stone, for I have allowed this to happen to you. Rama, can you ever forgive me?"

He didn't hear Kausalya's words that Rama's love for him was undiminished. Sumitra and Kausalya tried to soothe his ramblings, but he no longer seemed to be aware of them. He spoke only to Rama.

After some time, the two queens fell asleep by his side. By morning King Dasharatha was dead. He had not been able to live without Rama. His son had left him, propelled by the mission for which he had been born. Ravana's days were numbered, and Dasharatha's old heart could not bear waiting for his son's return.

Rama and Lakshmana did not know that they had left tragedy behind and that their beloved father could no longer persuade the blood to flow through his broken heart. The king died without them, as the curse prophesied. His son still had many years to live and many tasks to accomplish before he could return to his kingdom. No one heard the king's dying word, "Rama," least of all his beloved son, for Rama was at that moment deep in the forest.

Main Characters

Sun Dynasty

Rama's Family

Anaranya – King of the Sun-dynasty more than twenty-five generations

before Rama, killed by Ravana in a famous battle

Bharata –Rama's half-brother, second in line to the throne

Dasharatha – Emperor of the Earth, Rama's father, known for his great skill in battle

Trishanku –Rama's ancestor, whose very name Trishanku or Three Faults speaks of the king he was

Kaikeyi – Third and favorite wife of king Dasharatha, mother of Bharata

Kausalya – First wife of king Dasharatha, mother of Rama

Lakshmana – Rama's closest friend and half-brother

Rama – Firstborn son of king Dasharatha, wed to Sita, next in line to the throne

Shanta – Daughter of Kausalya and Dasharatha, adopted by king Romapada, married to Rishyasringa

Shatrugna - Lakshmana's twin-brother, Bharata's constant companion

Sumitra – Second wife of Dasharatha, mother of Lakshmana and Shatrugna

Vasishta – One of the nine manasa, mind-born, children of Brahma – the creator, the royal priest of the Sun Dynasty through countless generations

Sita's Family

Bhumi Devi – Mother Earth, considered as Sita's biological mother

Janaka – King of Mitthila, Sita's adoptive father who found Sita in a furrow

Kushadvaja – King Janaka's younger brother

Mandavi – Wife of Bharata, Sita's cousin, King Kushadvaja's daughter

Sita – Rama's wife who appeared from the Earth, adopted by King Janaka as his own, also known as Janaki

Srutakirti – Shatrugna's wife, Sita's cousin, King

Kushadvaja's daughter

Sunayana – King Janaka's wife, mother of Urmila

Urmila – Sita's sister, daughter of Janaka and Sunayana

Other Related Stories

(For those who are interested to learn more about the epic, here is additional history on some of the key characters from Krishna Dharma's *Ramayana*)

Ravana

A powerful leader of the Rakshasa race. His birth is described in Valmiki Ramayana as follows:

Long ago on the slopes of Mount Meru there lived a sage named Pulastya, who was a mind-born son of Brahma. He was constantly engaged in the practice of severe asceticism. Many celestial maidens would come to sport in the beautiful region where he dwelt, and they would often disturb his meditations. Finally becoming impatient with them, he said, "If any maiden should again be seen by me, she will immediately become pregnant."

The maidens then carefully avoided Pulastya's ashrama. However, there was one girl, a daughter of another sage named Trinabindu, who had not heard about the curse. She ventured into the region where Pulastya sat and as soon as he saw her she found indications of pregnancy in her body. Astonished and fearful, she ran to her father and said, "Father, I cannot understand why I am suddenly appearing as if pregnant. No contact with any male has ever been had by me."

Trinabindu sat in meditation and by his mystic power he understood what had happened. He then went with his daughter to Pulastya and said to him, "O venerable sage, kindly accept my daughter as your wife. By your power she now carries a child. Please therefore take her hand in marriage. She will surely render you very pleasing service."

Pulastya agreed and he said to the girl, "O gentle one, you will give birth to a highly qualified son who shall be known as Visrava."

Like his father, Visrava became an ascetic and engaged himself in much penance and study of scriptures. In due course he married a daughter of Bharadvaja and through her begot a son named Vaishravana, who by the grace of his father became the powerful Kuvera, the god of wealth.

At that time a great battle took place between the gods and the Rakshasas, who were finally put to flight by Vishnu. They sought shelter in the nether worlds, although one of them, Sumali, began to live on earth. As he wandered about he saw one day Kuvera flying overhead in the celestial Pushpaka chariot. The Rakshasa was astonished to see Kuvera's opulence. Knowing that the god was Visrava's son, and desiring to do good to the Rakshasas, he said to his young daughter Kaikasi, "It is high time you were wed, dear girl. Go quickly to Visrava's ashrama and ask that he accept you. That powerful sage will give you sons equal to the lord of riches; there is no doubt at all."

In obedience to her father, Kaikasi went to where Visrava was seated in meditation. She stood bashfully before him with folded palms, looking downward and scratching the earth with her toe. Seeing that girl, whose face resembled the full moon and who shone with a celestial beauty, the sage said, "Who are you and why are you here? Tell me the truth, O beautiful one"

The girl replied, "O sage, you should divine my purpose by your own mystic power, for I am too shy to tell you."

The sage meditated for some minutes and read her mind. He then said, "I have understood your purpose, O gentle one. You desire sons by me. Surely I am attracted to you and will accept your hand, but you have approached me at an inauspicious time. You will therefore have sons who will be cruel-minded, fierce-looking and given to evil deeds. O lady of shapely limbs, you will bring forth Rakshasas fond of drinking blood."

Kaikasi was upset. "O lordly sage, I do not desire such offspring. Kindly be merciful to me."

Feeling compassion, Visrava replied, "It cannot be any other way, dear girl, but I can bless you as follows. Although you will have such sons, your last son will be different. He will be virtuous and fully in accord with my family."

In due course Kaikasi gave birth to a hideous child with the form of a Rakshasa. He had ten heads, twenty hands, and was the color of coal. When he was born many inauspicious omens were seen. Vixens emitted flames from their mouths, blood fell from the sky, meteors dropped down and clouds thundered fiercely. The earth rocked with its load of mountains and the sea roared and sent up huge waves. Visrava named the child Dasagriva and he grew up fearful and cruel.

Next Kaikasi gave birth to Kumbhakarna, then Surpanakha, and finally Vibhishana. When this last son was born, flowers fell from the sky and the gods in heaven were heard to utter, "Good! Excellent!"

Some time after their birth Kuvera came on the Pushpaka to see his father. Seeing him blazing with glory and opulence, Kaikasi said to Dasagriva, "Son, you look here at your brother Vaisravana. Look at your self in comparison, so poor and lacking in power. Exert yourself so that you are the equal of your brother in every way."

Spurred on by his mother's words, Dasagriva said, "I swear to you that I shall rise equal to Vaisravana and even excel him in power. Do not grieve." In a mood of envy for his brother and greed for power, Dasagriva engaged himself in severe austerities for a very long time. In the end he won his famous boons from Brahma, being blessed that he could not be slain by any creature other than a man or lesser animal, for whom he had no regard whatsoever.

Along with Dasagriva, both Kumbhakarna and Vibhishana also engaged themselves in asceticism. When Brahma appeared before them, Vibhishana asked for the boon that his mind would always remain fixed in righteousness, even when he was in the greatest difficulty. Brahma granted his request and then turned toward Kumbhakarna to accord him a boon.

At that time the gods became greatly fearful and they approached Brahma, saying, "O lord, no boon at all should be granted by you to this one. He has already wrought havoc in the heavens, devouring seven Apsaras, ten attendants of the mighty Indra, as well as numerous seers and human beings.

What will he do if made powerful by a boon from yourself? On the pretext of granting a boon you should instead place him under a spell of delusion, thereby saving all the worlds from him."

Brahma smiled and said, "Be it so." He thought of the goddess of learning,

Sarasvati, and when she appeared before him he said to her, "O goddess, become the speech in Kumbhakarna's mouth."

The goddess agreed and Brahma then asked Kumbhakarna, "What boon do you desire, O Rakshasa?"

Kumbhakarna, weary from his austerities, replied, "Let me sleep for many years."

"It shall be so. You will sleep for six months at a time and remain awake for one day."

Having made his reply, Brahma vanished along with all the gods.

After receiving his boon, Dasagriva, who became known as Ravana, considered himself invincible. He went to Lanka, where Kuvera lived, and challenged his brother. On the advice of Visrava, Kuvera left the city and it was taken over by Ravana and his hordes of Rakshasa followers.

Sita

The daughter of King Janaka who became Rama's wife. How she was born on earth is described in a Vedic literature known as the Devi Bhagavata as follows:

There was once a great rishi called Kushadvaja who had a daughter named Vedavati, who was said to be an incarnation of the goddess Lakshmi.

Kushadvaja was petitioned by various celestials and demons for his daughter's hand, but she had set her mind on getting Vishnu as her husband.

One day a demon named Shambhu asked for Vedavati's hand in marriage, but he was refused. Becoming furious, he attacked and killed Kushadvaja. When Vedavati saw this she looked in anger at the demon and he was immediately burnt to ashes. She then went to the forest and began to meditate in order to propitiate Vishnu and get him as her husband. It was at that time that Ravana came there and insulted her, as described in the prologue of this book.

After she immolated her body, it is said that Ravana took her ashes with him back to Lanka. He kept them in a gold box in his palace. However, soon after this he saw many inauspicious omens in Lanka. The rishi Narada, on a visit to Lanka, informed Ravana that the cause of the ill omens was the presence of Vedavati's ashes. The demon then had them thrown into the ocean.

The box containing the ashes was carried by the ocean and deposited on the seashore near Mitthila. It went into the earth and it was at that place that Janaka performed a sacrifice for getting a child. A part of his sacrifice was the furrowing of the earth and he thus found the box. Lakshmi had entered the ashes, and when Janaka unearthed the box he found a golden child inside.

This child was named Sita.

Valmiki

The Ramayana's original author. The story of how he first came to compose the work is told in the Ramayana itself as follows:

One day Valmiki was visited in his ashrama by the celestial seer Narada. Valmiki asked him who was the most virtuous person in the world. Wanting to know if there was a perfect person anywhere, he asked, "Who is possessed of all power and knows what is right? Who is always truthful, firm of resolve and conscious of all services rendered? Who has subdued his self, conquered anger, is above fault-finding and, although being friendly to all beings, is nevertheless feared by even the gods when angry? O eminent sage, I have a great curiosity to know this and you are surely capable of telling me."

Actually, by his own spiritual practices and meditations Valmiki had been able to realise that the Supreme Lord, Vishnu, had appeared on the earth in

human form. He wanted Narada, whom he saw as a spiritual master, to tell him about the Lord's incarnation.

Narada replied, "There is one descended in the line of Iksvaku and known by men as Rama. He is powerful, radiant, resolute and has brought his senses under control. Intelligent, sagacious, eloquent, glorious and an exterminator of foes, he knows the secret of virtue, is true to his promise and is intent on the good of the people."

Narada went on at length describing Rama's many qualities. He then narrated in brief the whole story of Rama's pastimes. When he had finished he said, "This Rama is now ruling in Ayodhya. Indeed, you have already met him when he came to your ashrama. The remaining part of his pastimes are yet to be manifested. O sage, all this will soon be described by yourself. This sacred story of Rama, known as the Ramayana, should be heard by all men. It is on a par with the Vedas and capable of destroying all sins. Hearing or reading this narrative a man will, on departing from this world, be honored in heaven along with his sons, grandsons, followers and attendants."

Narada rose to leave and was worshipped by Valmiki. As the celestial seer rose into the sky by his mystic power, Valmiki stood thinking about Rama. He had already sensed his divinity when he met him some years back. Narada had confirmed his intuition. Feeling thrilled with transcendental ecstasy, Valmiki made his way toward the nearby river to take his midday bath, followed by his disciples.

As he went toward the riverbank, the rishi surveyed the beautiful forest scenery. He saw playing among the reeds by the river a pair of cranes. Those two birds were engaged in mating and they sported together making a delightful sound. Suddenly, as Valmiki looked on, a Nishada huntsman fired an arrow and struck one of the birds. Mortally wounded and covered in blood, it thrashed about on the ground screaming in pain. Its mate also cried piteously and fell about in sorrow.

Seeing this, the soft-hearted Valmiki felt compassion. He saw the Nishada approaching with bow in hand. In grief, he said to that hunter, "As you have slain this poor bird while it was absorbed in pleasure, may you have no peace of mind for the rest of your life."

The curse came out in perfectly metered poetry. Astonished by this, Valmiki said, "What have I uttered? Tormented by grief I have composed a stanza filled with that emotion."

The sage, brooding over the incident, entered the river and took his bath. After coming out he went back to his hermitage still thinking on the rhyming couplet he had spoken to the hunter. When he reached his ashrama he took his seat and was about to commence his lessons to his disciples when Brahma suddenly appeared there. Seeing the great creator of the universe approaching on his swan carrier, Valmiki hastily rose and joined his palms in humility. He offered his prostrate obeisances and worshipped the deity with many prayers. Brahma then sat down on an exalted seat quickly brought for him by Valmiki's students.

Even though Brahma was present before him, Valmiki could not stop thinking about the incident with the hunter. He again recited the verse he had composed. Feeling sorry that he had lost control of himself, he appeared dejected and sighed.

Brahma laughed and said, "Let this poetic utterance of yours become the source of your glory. Do not brood any more, O sage. It was by my arrangement that this speech flowed from your lips. In that same meter you

should now describe the pastimes on earth of the all-wise Rama. Tell the story of that hero as you have heard it from Narada. By my mercy you will be able to see every detail of that story, as clearly as a fruit held in the palm of your hand. Therefore, render this sacred and soul-ravishing tale into verse for the good of the world."

Brahma blessed the sage that his narrative would remain extant for as long as the mountains stood on the face of the earth. He also told him that he would be able to continue living anywhere he chose within the universe for the same length of time.

Having finished speaking, Brahma disappeared. Valmiki was filled with wonder. He and his disciples gazed in amazement at Brahma's seat for some time. Gradually regaining their presence of mind, the sage's students began reciting the verse he had uttered to the hunter. They were overjoyed at the honor bestowed upon Valmiki by Brahma. The sage then began to meditate on Rama's pastimes, gradually composing the Ramayana over the coming days.

Author's Note

THE QUESTION OF authorship of the Ramayana is somewhat problematic because the story of Rama existed long before I did. The hero in this tale, Prince Rama, has been hailed as the perfect gentleman, valiant and gentle. Originating in India, his life and adventures have been told and re-told and have been the subject of much debate. "Was he really a perfect hero?" the less enamored ask. Perfect or not, the conception of Rama's gentle nature has earned him a large following of worshippers.

In Hindi they sing, *Sab kuch dede Rama, Sab kuch mange Shyam*—Rama will give you all you wish for, while Shyam, Krsna, takes from you all that you have. Krsna is of course another well-loved figure in India, whose character is, as the song above hints, in many ways opposite to Rama. Rama, as a character, a hero, a god, is a well-established figure in India and elsewhere. Because the foundation of Rama's story already existed, I consider myself only an interpreter. Like filling in the colors in a coloring book where the outline has already been made, my attempt has been to choose a suitable color-scheme.

The *Ramayana* was written ages ago in Sanskrit, but it has since been rewritten and retold in most of the other languages of the Indian subcontinent and indeed of Asia. Interestingly, very few of the hundreds of written versions have been close translations of Valmiki's *Ramayana.* Instead the storytellers have permitted themselves considerable liberty in depicting characters and even changed or omitted basic details of the story. The debates that I mentioned previously have also given rise to 'anti-works' where, for example, Ravana, the antagonist, has been made into the hero. These interpretations, and other more favorable ones, are based primarily on Valmiki's *Ramayana* but they have a different purpose or message. What those purposes might be are subject to scholarly debate; my interest in the Ramayana has been far removed from these in-depth queries.

Indeed, my exposure to the *Ramayana* began when I was too young to ask questions. Stories from the *Mahabharata,* the *Bhagavat Purana,* and *Ramayana* were not only my bed-time stories but the stories of my childhood. Even as an adult, they retain a sense of inherent familiarity, and the characters are to me as near and dear as any family member would be. I feel that I understand the characters and their motives and, thus, have the right to question their actions. Most notably, I have written from memory, naturally giving rise to a certain amount of interpretation. Naturally, the question of authenticity was ever-present in my mind, and the use of creativity or imagination while writing felt uneasy, even contrary to the 'intellectual chastity' inculcated in me.

However, when I started cross-referencing what I had written, I discovered that 'my version' – the one I was raised on – was already a mix between the Kamban's Tamil *Iramavataram* and the *Valmiki Ramayana,* two prominent versions, the latter considered by some the original. This discovery allowed me to question the very idea of authenticity. I feel now that the many regional versions cannot simply be dismissed, for they have been adapted to make sense to their particular audience.

Now that I have explained my rationale for implementing changes in the text, I will be more specific about where the major embellishments occur. Those who are already familiar with the *Ramayana* will be able to discern where I have elaborated; my hope is that they will also see the reason for it.

In the section on Rama's childhood, I have taken more liberties, due to the scarcity of information in any of the older versions. For example, from the mention in the *Kamban Ramayana* that Manthara disliked Rama because as a child he had thrown mud on her, I developed Chapter Six entitled 'A Dirty Fight'. Some other chapters, however, I must admit, cannot be traced in this way, for they are taken from my imagination. For the sake of clarity (and for the conscientious reader), I list the sections which are not found in the ancient texts but are my creations alone:

Chapter Two – An Earnest Wish

Chapter Five – A Son is Born

Chapter Six – A Dirty Fight

Chapter Seven – A Mother's Morning

The rest of this book's content can be found in a similar form in any of the old texts. Otherwise I have been faithful to 'my version', i.e. my peculiar mix of *Kamban* and *Valmiki Ramayana.* Most dialogues, in fact, are close paraphrases of those found in these 'original' versions.

Nevertheless, as will be visible to those who have read the *Ramayana* before, this book remains my interpretation. I can only pray that by interpreting it as I have, the events and characters will be easier to relate to and to understand for the young reader.

JAICO PUBLISHING HOUSE

Elevate Your Life. Transform Your World.

ESTABLISHED IN 1946, Jaico Publishing House is home to world-transforming authors such as Sri Sri Paramahansa Yogananda, Osho, The Dalai Lama, Srì Sri Ravi Shankar, Sadhguru, Robin Sharma, Deepak Chopra, Jack Canfield, Eknath Easwaran, Devdutt Pattanaik, Khushwant Singh, John Maxwell, Brian Tracy and Stephen Hawking.

Our late founder Mr. Jaman Shah first established Jaico as a book distribution company. Sensing that independence was around the corner, he aptly named his company Jaico ('Jai' means victory in Hindi). In order to service the significant demand for affordable books in a developing nation, Mr. Shah initiated Jaico's own publications. Jaico was India's first publisher of paperback books in the English language.

While self-help, religion and philosophy, mind/body/spirit, and business titles form the cornerstone of our non-fiction list, we publish an exciting range of travel, current affairs, biography, and popular science books as well. Our renewed focus on popular fiction is evident in our new titles by a host of fresh young talent from India and abroad. Jaico's recently established Translations Division translates selected English content into nine regional languages.

Jaico's Higher Education Division (HED) is recognized for its student-friendly textbooks in Business Management and Engineering which are in use countrywide.

In addition to being a publisher and distributor of its own titles, Jaico is a major national distributor of books of leading international and Indian publishers. With its headquarters in Mumbai, Jaico has branches and sales offices in Ahmedabad, Bangalore, Bhopal, Bhubaneswar, Chennai, Delhi, Hyderabad, Kolkata and Lucknow.

SINCE 1946